HOW TO KNOW GOD'S WILL

HOW TO
KNOW
God's Will

BY CHARLES W. SHEPSON

Horizon House Publishers
Beaverlodge, Alberta, Canada

HORIZON BOOKS
are published by Horizon House Publishers
Box 600, Beaverlodge, Alberta TOH OCO
Printed in the United States of America

Unless otherwise noted, biblical quotations are
from the *New International Version*, copyright ©
1978 by New York International Bible Society.
Used by permission.

TO MY DEAREST FRIEND
whose guidance, love,
understanding, and patience
have enriched my life
more than I could ever fully appreciate,
much less express.

Proverbs 18:24
John 15:15
Psalm 32:8
John 15:9
John 21:15-17

CONTENTS

> *To many Christians, God's will is an elusive plan securely hidden by God and discovered only after a diligent search—if then. Why is this so?*

The Desire to Know the Will of God / Reasons For So Strongly Desiring to Know the Will of God / Man's Distorted Impression of God's Will / The Importance of Really Wanting the Will of God

> *God delights to use a variety of methods to lead His children.*

God Leads By Closed Doors / By Remarkable Revelations / By Difficult Experiences / By Specific Instructions / By Sanctified Reason / By the Counsel of Godly People / By Devotional Application / By Open Doors / By Inner Peace

How God used each of the above methods to lead the author to begin an unusual ministry.

There are specific steps you can take to discover God's will for your life.

Clarify your concept of God / Memorize Scripture that reflects His nature / Memorize Scripture that promises you a revelation of His will / Follow His revealed will now / Refuse to fear the revelation of God's will / Be certain you sincerely want His will / Read your Bible consistently / Ask God to fill you with His Holy Spirit / Exercise your faith / Weigh the circumstances / Specifically ask Him to reveal His will to you / Obey step by step what He reveals / Test your proposed decision by submitting it to godly Christians who know you well / Don't let reverses shake your confidence

A review of the ways God leads, with faith-building glimpses into the will of God at work in twentieth-century lives.

PREFACE

God has enriched my life immeasurably through the clear communication of His will for me. I sincerely believe that He *enjoys* communicating clearly with His own. I believe He *wants* to show *you* His will for *your* life, as well.

The illustrative material I present may prove inspirational and even entertaining in the better sense of that word, but I have tried not to lose sight of my primary goal of instruction. The "how to" element is designedly woven throughout the book.

For too many years, Christians were told "to" without being instructed "how to." I delight to see more and more instructional material available now.

During my thirty years of preaching, I have coveted the comment, "I *learned* something from that message, pastor," rather than the oft repeated and sometimes fruitless statement, "I *enjoyed* that message, pastor."

May it please God both to *teach* you *AND* to give you pleasure through the reading of this book!

Section I

GOD'S WILL
How Elusive is It?

I was bone weary! Weariness was not the only feeling in my bones, however. There were deeply satisfying emotions as well. There was a sense of accomplishment. There was a thrill of excitement over the imagined startled look on my parents' faces when they would discover what I had done for them. There was the electrifying sense of being fully alive that comes from doing something "different." How could I know that these feelings would be overshadowed within the next hour as effectively as if we were to put Mount Rainier alongside our own four thousand foot Holston Mountain?

In a hectic yesterday I had completed the complicated registration process at Nyack College with uncharacteristic speed. With registration out of the way, I knew it was possible for me to accomplish the project for my parents in a single day if I rose with the roosters. I negotiated the 50 mile bus-subway-bus trip to my home in Cranford, New Jersey, with such beautiful synchronization that it seemed almost

11

as if the three vehicles were running just for my convenience. This was *my* day! No question about it!

My parents were away enjoying a few days of vacation. I worked feverishly at my skills, so often applied to the homes of others, but this time used to surprise my own parents. If the wallpaper would cooperate and stay where I put it without stretching, if the match would prove somewhat uncomplicated, if the quality brushes I had purchased would serve as well as I hoped they would for the painting of the woodwork, I could possibly complete their entire bedroom before the day was over.

Everything went smoothly!

When the last strip of wallpaper hung in place, and the last brushful of paint gleamed on the baseboard, and the tools were cleaned and stored, there was hardly time for one more admiring look before dashing to the "Star Route" bus that linked my hometown with the Port Authority terminal in New York City.

There was a definite similarity between the sound of the "clunk" of my fifty-cent piece in the change box on the bus, and the "plunk" of my 125 pounds as I fell into my seat. I leaned my head back against the headrest and drew in three times the usual breath, holding it momentarily. Why does that feel so good when you think you are more tired than you have ever been in all your life?

It was 10:03. I raised my watch arm rather than my head, and studied the face. Simple math stumbled in my brain. After a day like this one, my calculations were far from calculator-like in speed. As a matter of fact, they were even a far cry from the old whirring, jerking, lurching Friden calculators I used to operate. But if the driver would concentrate on the road, and the traffic lights between Cranford and New York City would cooperate, and not too many customers would force a stop, and the "A" train subway express would come at just the right moment, I might make that eleven p.m. bus from upper Manhattan to Nyack.

And if not? The next bus would leave at midnight, one long hour later. "Midnight!" That sounded more ominous than usual.

I must have checked my watch 52 times in half as many minutes while the bus sped toward New York City. Yes, it *was* my day! Everything was falling into place beautifully: the lights, the traffic, the people, the driver, and even the hands on my watch.

When the bus lurched to a stop in the Port Authority terminal, I was the first one out through those fold-away doors. I dashed down the subway steps with reckless abandon. I could hear the clackety-clatter of the arriving train in the tunnel below. I may even have negotiated three steps at a time in my hurry. At any rate, I was able to squeeze through those closing doors of the subway train, and to flop on one of the seats, panting, but delighted with my continuing good fortune.

The next few minutes were tense ones. The subway would have to travel right along, or I would still miss that bus. I knew those stops well:

59th Street, 72nd Street, 125th Street, etc. 59th Street arrived in less time than I had allotted. "Three cheers!" I said to myself. The next stop was ahead of schedule as well. "Thank you, Lord," I prayed in my heart, aware that God had been especially good to me in every way that day.

Hold everything! Something seemed ominously wrong about that last stop. I felt it almost instinctively. As the doors were closing I caught a glimpse of the station identification imbedded in the tiled walls. They were definitely not a seven and a two! The impact of my error struck me forcibly. This was not the "A" express hurtling toward the George Washington Bridge. It was the "D" express following the same tracks as the "A" train as far as 59th Street, and then veering off into the Bronx!

Painfully aware of the consequences of such an error, I got off at the next station, and took a south-bound "D" train back to 59th Street. There I crossed to the north-bound platform to get the next "A" express that would come along.

Dejected, I looked at my watch again. This wasn't my day after all—not all the way through, anyway. There was no possibility of making that bus to Nyack now, *unless it was late*. The doors were hardly open widely enough at 175th Street when I forced my body through them and dashed up the stairs into the terminal just in time to watch the taillights of my bus to Nyack going down the street in the direction of the George Washington Bridge.

If I had been 30 seconds earlier, I would have been praising the Lord for delaying that bus long enough for me to catch it. What was I to think now? It seems Romans 8:28 gets overworked at times. When you are as tired as I was, it isn't all that easy to glibly spout, "Praise the Lord anyhow!" Oh well, it certainly wasn't the end of the world. In another 55 minutes the midnight bus would be leaving for Nyack. It would be childish to get too upset. But when you are tired in every muscle it is a bit difficult to act mature!

At 11:30 I walked out to the slot from which the Nyack bus would be leaving. "If I'm this early, I may as well get in line and enjoy a good seat," I reasoned. Standing there, I noticed a motherly older woman who appeared to be Scandinavian come to stand right behind me. There was something so wholesome and gracious about her that I wondered if she knew the Lord Jesus too. I asked her a question I very seldom ask anyone, for the term is often misunderstood: "Are you a Christian?"

"Why, yes!" she exlaimed, "I *am* a Christian." After some joyous visiting together, I noticed a thoughtful squinting of her blue eyes as she asked me pointedly, "Where are you going?"

"To Nyack," I replied.

"And when you arrive in Nyack, where are you going?"

"Up the hill to the college," I responded.

"Oh, praise the Lord!" she exclaimed sincerely with delight written all over her Swedish face. "I too am going up the hill to visit my brother, Dr. Lee Olson. I knew I had to walk through a section of town that frightens me on my

15

way up the hill, so I prayed and asked the Lord Jesus to send someone to walk with me.''

Suddenly Romans 8:28 no longer seemed overworked or the least bit inappropriate. The glory of the living God and His interest in our lives was so very evident. God does indeed have a perfect plan for our lives. It even includes getting on the wrong train so you *will* miss the 11 o'clock bus when there is a prayer to be answered on the 12 o'clock bus! That took the weariness out of my bones. When I arrived in my dormitory room at nearly 1 a.m. I felt the exhilaration of a day never-to-be-forgotten, rather than the bone-weariness of a few hours earlier.

God's will, beautifully revealed and sweetly accomplished, had added a rare perfume to that day's memory that would overshadow forever the odors of wet wallpaper and fresh latex paint! I am certain that every Christian would enjoy that kind of evident intervention in his life proving God's personal interest.

THE DESIRE TO KNOW THE WILL OF GOD

A longing to be led by God specifically in at least the more important details of life, seems to be a basic instinct of the truly born again person. In my counseling experience, the question of knowing the will of God either for making an investment of the life, or for a momentary situation, seems to dominate.

Bill Bright, founder and president of Campus Crusade for Christ International says, ''One of the questions that I am most frequently asked is, "How can I know God's will for my life?" [1]

Paul Little, in his booklet "Affirming the Will of God," suggests that if a person had one question he might ask of the Lord Jesus with a guarantee of an immediate answer, he would probably ask one related in some way to God's will for his life! [2]

This suggestion that God's will is probably uppermost in your mind is confirmed by a homework assignment I gave each year for ten years at the St. Paul Bible College. The class was Homiletics (how to preach), and the students were prospective preachers. I listed twenty sermon titles for them, all very revealing of the content of the sermon. They were titles like these:

"How Soon May We Expect Christ's Return?"
"Where Did We Get Our Bible?"
"How to Make Your Faith Increase"
"How to Rise Above Depression"
"How to Have Meaningful Devotions"
"What is Heaven Like?"
"What Makes a Happy Home?"
"How to Share Your Faith Effectively"
"How to Know the Will of God for Your Life"

There were eleven other titles as well. I asked the students to list their selections in the order of importance to them, and to choose only ten. Every year, without exception, "How to Know the Will of God for Your Life" ran away with the number one position.

Paul Little, in his excellent booklet previously referred to, insists that the vast majority of the will of God for your life has already been revealed in the Bible.[3] Dr. A.W. Tozer states in his pamphlet entitled "How the Lord Leads," that the matters which require some special guidance from the Lord to prevent us from making serious mistakes are "few and rare."[4] If these statements are accurate, *why* is this issue of the will of God for a person's life such a big one with sincere Christians? Why does finding His will for our lives become almost an obsession?

REASONS FOR SO STRONGLY DESIRING TO KNOW THE WILL OF GOD

First: We know almost instinctively that God's will for us is "good, pleasing and perfect" (Romans 12:2). After all, knowing what God's personality is like leads us to that conclusion. The more we know God, therefore, the more we long to know also His perfect will for us.

Second: We are aware both instinctively and through God's clear teaching in Scripture that being led by the Spirit of God is a confirmation of our relationship to Him. "Those who are led by the Spirit of God are sons of God," He has said.[5] We want that kind of reassurance that we are *really* His.

Third: We know from experience that following our own will leads to a mixed diet of sweet and sour life experiences. Even King David, who was called in the Bible "a man after (God's) own heart"[6] had moments of deep heartache and remorse looking back upon times in his life when he had chosen his own way instead of God's perfect will for him.

Fourth: We are haunted by the thought that we have "Only one life, 'twill soon be past, (and) only what's done for Christ will last."[7] That thought is not only familiar poetry, but also frightening promise from God. We are assured that the quality of our living will be tested severely, and the trivial and temporal aspects will be burned up.[8]

Fifth: We love God and want to please Him. Pleasing God is accomplished in part by doing His will, according to His own statement that "If you love me you will obey what I command."[9] Paul prayed for the New Testament believers earnestly that they might "be filled with the knowledge of His will...to lead a life worthy of the Lord, fully pleasing to Him."[10]

Sixth: In one measure or another, the fear of failure is with us all. We want to be successful, and we realize that "success" is linked with obedience to the will of God. The promise of God is that "If you fully obey the Lord your God and carefully follow all his commands I give you today....All these blessings will come upon you and accompany you...."[11] A long list of blessings follows in the next twelve verses. The passage is written to the nation of Israel, but on the strength of I Corinthians 10:11 which makes it clear that Israel was one grand object lesson for today's Christians, we can properly make personal application. God *will* bless us wonderfully with success *if* we follow His will. We need to know His will to follow it.

Seventh: We know that living under God's moment by moment guidance would add a dimension of purposefulness and meaning to our lives that we could never achieve by ourselves. When we think this issue through, we agree with Dr. Dwight Carlson that, "Living God's will is the greatest thing that can ever happen to you." [12]

A service station mechanic in Brunswick, Nebraska, was sprawled underneath a car when he thought he heard the footsteps of David Modlin passing through his garage on his way home from school. "Is that you, David? How would you like to go to camp this summer at Rivercrest?"

"I'd like to," David responded, "but I guess I couldn't afford to." His well-worn clothes backed up his statement effectively. The mechanic knew the truth of that; he was aware that David's mother worked as a bar maid, and that her earnings hardly warranted her absence from the home. "I'll pay your way if your mom will let you go," he called to David from under the car. David ran to ask his mom about it. In short order he was back to report with excitement that his mom had said he could go.

The mechanic sent David's registration in immediately, judging by his size that he would be a junior camper. That judgment was both wrong and right! It was "wrong" as to which camp the regulations said David belonged in. It was "right" as to God's perfect will. David arrived at Rivercrest a week earlier than he would have without that error. All through the week, in addition to the sports and the swimming and the crafts and the fun times with the other campers, David attended the meetings in the big tent each evening and heard the nightly evangelistic messages. Night after night while others responded to the invitations, David resisted God and would not receive the Lord Jesus personally.

When the final night came, almost everyone in camp was praying for David, the holdout! I gave the invitation that night after preaching the final evangelistic sermon of the week. I noticed that David's counselor left his seat and went over to David and quietly talked with him. I saw David's head shake a definite "No." Then something happened that caused a lot of people to wince. A mentally retarded boy who had also been praying for David left his seat and walked over to where David stood. He took David by the hand and literally pulled him to the altar, and pushed him down on his knees in the sawdust. We all realized what an unfortunate thing had happened...*but we were all wrong!*

There at that altar in Fremont, Nebraska, David began to cry. A counselor in a gracious manner and with ease led the boy to Christ. After the service I saw him lingering under one of the tent flaps. I went over to him and asked, "What happened to you tonight, David?" With tears of joy he told me that he had received the Lord Jesus into his life as his Savior from sin. "Let me have your Bible, David," I said. In the front of it I entered the date and wrote these words, "Tonight, I, David Modlin, received the Lord

Jesus into my heart and life here at the Rivercrest Bible Camp in Fremont, Nebraska.'' I asked him to sign his name to that statement on the flyleaf of his Bible. We prayed together, and my heart rejoiced along with his.

The next day David returned home from camp. That afternoon he went for a swim in the water-filled old quarry pits and drowned! Three days later, at that little boy's funeral, they read the eternally significant statement on the flyleaf of his Bible.

David is in heaven today because a faithful mechanic fulfilled the will of God by acting upon God's prompting to send him to camp. He is there because God led that man to send him to the wrong camp, one week too early (he would have drowned before leaving for the next camp). He is there because a mentally retarded boy who loved the Lord Jesus did what God prompted him to do. Eternal salvation for David was effected because God could lead His children in *very* specific ways.

There is no question but that living under God's moment by moment guidance adds immeasurably to the effectiveness of a person's life. Dr. Sidlow Baxter wrote,

Inside the will of God is the only place of full blessing. I will not go so far as to say that outside of direct guidance there is no blessing, for God graciously accepts all well meaning labor in His name, and often overrules it to good effect, but there cannot be full blessing, because it does not coincide

22

in detail with the predesigned pattern. Only when we are inside of the will of God by complete yieldedness can we with certainty do just the right thing in just the right way at just the right time and with just the intended result.... [13]

The Bible tells us that "God wanted to make the unchanging nature of His purpose very clear to the heirs of what was promised...." [14] His nature has not changed. He still wants to make His purposes very clear to us, and both the purposes (God's will) and the Author of those purposes (God Himself) do not change!

"We are God's workmanship, created in Christ Jesus to do good works, which God prepared in advance for us to do." [15] The Old and New Testament books are filled with instances where God told His people what He wanted them to do in specific terms, sometimes changing the entire course of their lives. Abraham was told to move to another country. Joseph was directed into Egypt and then at a precise time back into Galilee. The Apostle Paul was led to go to certain places and was kept from going to other places by God's deliberate interventions. God *does* have a plan for your life.

We love to hear that! Perhaps that is one of the reasons for the immense effectiveness of the Four Spiritual Laws booklet. That captivating first law reaches man where his greatest longings are: "God LOVES you, and offers a wonderful PLAN for your life." [16]

A primary goal of mine in this book is to help

you understand that *God delights to reveal His will to you.* That conviction runs counter to widespread ideas and attitudes prevailing among Christians, however. In the thinking of many, God's will is an elusive plan securely hidden by God and discovered only after a diligent search—*if then.* The pursuit of the will of God becomes a spiritual treasure hunt in which one follows puzzling and often ambiguous clues. Few find themselves on the winning team in this treasure hunt. Inside the persons holding such views, a frustration mounts as life steadily flows from the top of the hour glass to the bottom, and irretrievably time ebbs away. Life gets increasingly shorter, and God refuses to talk!

I object! That is not a picture of *my* God. Nor is it a proper reflection of the God of the Bible.

The God of the Bible clearly promises, "I will instruct you and teach you in the way you should go; I will counsel you and watch over you."[17] In an even more dramatic promise, God told the people of Jerusalem of His willingness to guide His people: "Your ears will hear a voice behind you saying, this is the way, walk in it."[18]

MAN'S DISTORTED IMPRESSION OF GOD'S WILL

We desire to know His will. *He is willing to reveal* His will. What stands in the way?

For some, there is a distorted conception of what God's will for them would be like. This is true in spite of the fact that He has already declared it to be "good, pleasing and perfect." [19]

In effect we are saying, "Let *me* be the judge of that!" when we fear to discover what His will is for us. If we search for it in a half-hearted way, nurturing ambivalent feelings of longing to know it on the one hand, fearing to find it to be something we do not want to do on the other hand, we are in effect slandering His great character. God loves us too much to will for us anything that is not in our very best interest. Why should I fear what is in my best interest?

Bill Bright reminds us that the Bible reveals God as loving, wise, merciful, all-knowing, all-powerful, and yet gracious. He concludes, "The man who has this view of God will have no trouble saying, 'Lord, I trust you with every detail and area of my life. Do what you want with me.' " [20]

From man's point of view, one of the worst things that could happen to a person is to lose his life. Yet Jim Elliott, one of the five missionaries martyred in Ecuador in 1954, referred to the "sheer joy of doing the will of God." [21] It is true that he did not know when he wrote those words that for him the pathway of the perfect will of God would lead to death on a sandbar at the end of an Auca spear. Yet had he known, I believe he would have been among the first to remind us that the martyr is specially favored of God, and privileged to be honored in heaven! With a loud voice, such persons will be referred to in heaven as those who " overcame him by the blood of the lamb and by the word of their testimony; they did not love their lives so much as to shrink from death.

25

Therefore rejoice, you heavens and you who dwell in them.''[22]

Some people seem to be certain that if they find God's will for them, it will include difficult tasks, great heartaches, unpleasant moments. They struggle between wanting to know His will and fearing what it might include. They speak of "surrendering to the will of God" as though that would be the ultimate accomplishment of submission. I find the very expression "surrendering to the will of God" distasteful. In a proper concept of the will of God, there should be no big struggle involving the ultimate raising of a white flag of surrender. A proper understanding of God's nature will help us anticipate His will with joy. "Embracing the will of God" suits me better than "surrendering to the will of God." With joy I should hold it close to my heart as a priceless, untarnishing treasure, a gift from the hand of the person who has more love for me than does anyone else in the universe!

I choose to believe God when He says that His will is "good" for me, and will be "pleasing" to me, and is "perfect" for me in every last detail. I do not mean to say that I believe every aspect of God's will for me will be beautifully pleasant. I only affirm that it is "good" and "perfect" and is ultimately "pleasing."

When God did not answer my prayer for healing and allowed me to go through extremely serious surgery to accomplish the deliverance from death and the new lease on life that I needed, I felt a keen sense of disappointment. He

26

could have spared me those three months in a body cast (neck to knees!) in the hottest months of the year, and without air-conditioning! One touch of the divine hand that still has all its ancient skill would have accomplished painlessly what the doctors so painstakingly and painmakingly did. Yet He chose for me the path of pain and suffering, of hospitalization and bedfastness. How glad I am that He did! In no other way could I have been prepared so thoroughly for the bedside ministry I have had to thousands of people during these thirty years of pastoral ministry.

I see clearly now that God has a curriculum for each one He receives into His training school. He customizes that curriculum to each one for the ultimate contribution to his usefulness in the kingdom. We must get passing grades in each course He prescribes, or the course has to be repeated. My God-ordered training for ministry was far more significant than the training I received at Nyack College and the universities (though I sincerely appreciate both). The Teacher of God's courses was the most gracious and tender and loving of all my teachers, and so personally interested in me!

God knows what is best for us. We do not need to fear His will. Fear is an affront to God. It indicates that we do not really know Him very well. "But I don't understand why God..."—how many times I have heard those words! We don't have to understand fully His purposes, we only need to trust them.

When the atomic bomb was being developed,

certain companies were asked to design a machine according to a mathematical formula which they did not fully understand. Those factories that followed the pattern submitted to them by the staff of atomic scientists learned eventually that they had been working smoothly within an overall plan that was to honor their nation. We may not fully understand God's formula, but if we follow it closely, when the final chapters are written, we will certainly discover that we have been living and serving within a framework carefully designed to greatly glorify our God.

Dr. Donald Barnhouse wrote about a Mississippi River steamer that was racing through the fog with the terrified passengers lining the rail. A committee appointed by the frightened passengers was sent to the bridge to rebuke the captain for his recklessness. They discovered that it was perfectly clear on the bridge! Dr. Barnhouse suggests that the next time we find ourselves in a fog, we should remind ourselves that God is *never* in a fog! [23] God knows full well what He is doing at all times. We need to be unswervingly convinced of that in order to have an undistorted impression of His will for us.

THE IMPORTANCE OF REALLY WANTING THE WILL OF GOD

There is great danger in an attitude that expresses itself like this: "Lord, I want to know Your will so that I can decide whether or not to follow it." I suspect that is the very reason God does not choose to reveal His will to some of us. Why should He submit a plan to us for our approval or disapproval? He would be contributing to our sinfulness if we should choose not to follow it!

In almost all writing on this subject, the authors sound the same note. George Muller, that legendary man of faith, wrote, "Nine-tenths of the difficulties are overcome when our hearts are ready to do the Lord's will, whatever it may be. When one is truly in this state, it is usually but a little way to the knowledge of what His will is."[24]

Dr. Barnhouse writes, "We must be willing to do His will before we know what it is."[25]

Paul Little feels that the most crucial prerequisite for special guidance is "to be willing to accept the will of God in these unspecified areas of our lives before we know what it is."[26]

What each has said, in effect, is that we must really want God's will regardless of what it contains in its details. Our commitment to the will of God must be thorough and without reservation. It should be as though He were to hand us a blank sheet of paper for us to sign, with the understanding that He would fill in the details of the contract after we had signed!

It may well be that this commitment without reservation is the most important step in the direction of ascertaining the will of God for our lives. Unless this issue is firmly settled, even the reading of this book could be a waste of your time and might even add to your sense of frustration.

In the following sections we will present: (1) ways in which the Lord leads His own, (2) a recent example of divine guidance that clearly reveals that our God plans in detail, (3) a check-list of items that can assist you in determining the will of God for your life, and (4) some faith-building glimpses into the will of God at work in twentieth century lives.

Section II

GOD'S WILL
How Does He Reveal It?

It seems strange that the same experience that can send a thrill of excitement up my spine can also send a chill of resentment down my spine! Well, maybe I shouldn't say the "same" experience. Perhaps I should call it a "similar" experience.

What do I dislike so strongly? A familiarity with God that expresses itself like this (and I am quoting!): "So God said to me, 'Just hang in there, Buddy; you ain't seen nuthin' yet!' " I find myself totally unimpressed by such an assertion. To be frank with you, I am somewhat nauseated!

That very experience, however (God speaking to His children clearly, intimately, and to the point), excites me tremendously! And when He does speak so definitely, I find that His English is flawless and His manner is dignified, as you might expect from such an incomparable Person.

God *loves* to speak to us. He *wants* to lead us. He wills to reveal His desires to His sincere children. If we are regularly reading the Bible, and are sensitive to His voice, we will thrill over how specifically and clearly He indicates His will for us. Remember that one of the basic premises of this book is that GOD DELIGHTS TO REVEAL HIS WILL TO HIS OWN.

By what methods does God lead? May we expect an audible voice? Surely God's will isn't written out for each Christian and handed to him! In this section we will remind you of a number of the ways by which God has led in the past (and still leads). This listing is not meant to be exhaustive but it will illustrate the great variety which is so characteristic of our God in all that He does.

GOD LEADS BY CLOSED DOORS

The most dramatic roadblock recorded in God's Word was an angel that was seen by a donkey, and was not seen by the man who was riding on that donkey!

> Balaam got up in the morning, saddled his donkey and went with the princes of Moab. But God was very angry when he went, and the angel of the Lord stood in the road to oppose him....When the donkey saw the angel of the Lord standing in the road with a drawn sword in his hand, she turned off the road into a field. Balaam beat her to get her back on the road.

Two more times the angel blocked the way, and each time Balaam beat his donkey.

Then the Lord opened the donkey's mouth, and she said to Balaam, "What have I done to you to make you beat me these three times?" Balaam answered the donkey, "You have made a fool of me! If I had a sword in my hand, I would kill you right now." The donkey said to Balaam, "Am I not your own donkey, which you have always ridden, to this day? Have I been in the habit of doing this to you?" "No," he said. Then the Lord opened Balaam's eyes, and he saw the angel of the Lord standing in the road with his sword drawn. So he bowed low and fell face down. [27]

A talking animal! That surely hasn't happened very often. But *roadblocks* are familiar to all of us. We have to remind ourselves that God's stops are sometimes designed to serve as stepping stones, and that "delay" does not necessarily spell "denial."

When I was a shy, somewhat insecure teenager, God used a roadblock to prepare me for His service. I saw it as keeping me from preparation for His service at the time, but I was very wrong. I longed to go to Bible college to train for the ministry. Sickness, financial reverses, and family problems combined to work against that longing, and I had to go to work in a chemical factory for three years. Now I look back upon those three years and thank God for them. There were some courses in God's curriculum that were not offered in any of the Bible colleges, and He wanted me to take some of those first. God has a purpose in every closed door.

GOD LEADS BY REMARKABLE REVELATIONS

Through a vision on a rooftop, God led Peter. Three men from Joppa were approaching Peter's house to ask him to come to the home of Cornelius, who was a Gentile, to share the good news. He would never have gone with them without specific directions from God ordering him to violate deeply entrenched Jewish traditions.

Peter saw something like a large sheet full of unclean animals and birds let down from heaven. A voice said, "Get up, Peter, kill and eat." Peter answered, "Surely not, Lord, I have never eaten anything impure or unclean." "Do not call anything impure that God has made clean," the voice insisted. When the men arrived, Peter was ready and willing to go with them, prepared by the vision God had given to him. [28]

Visions...I don't think they happen frequently either. God does use them on occasion, however. Carolyn Eckman, Christian and Missionary Alliance missionary to Irian Jaya, Indonesia, awakened one night from a terrifying dream. In her horrible dream, she was driving along the tortuous two-lane road that leads to the coastal city of Jayapura. She came to a section of road that was being repaired. Only one lane of traffic was open and it led around a tight, blind curve. A spray of yellow-green bamboo overhung the road on the left side.

Just as she came to the curve (in her dream) a blue Volkswagen minibus with yellow taxicab license plates came hurtling around the curve. The two vehicles crashed head-on, scattering car and body parts all over the road! The horrifying vividness of the dream made returning to sleep very difficult.

The next afternoon Carolyn was in her car on her way to Jayapura where she helped new missionaries with their language study each week. She came to a blind curve. Repairs had reduced the road to one lane. She noticed the bright yellow-green of bamboo to the left. It was the same curve she had seen in her dream the night before, and the horrifying vividness of that dream all came before her sharply. She pulled as far off the road as she could get! Suddenly, screeching around that blind corner came a blue Volkswagen minibus with yellow taxicab license plates. It would certainly have hit her if she had not pulled off the road and stopped. God had spared her life by way of a dream! God does still use dreams and visions occasionally to lead His people.

I agree with Dr. Bill Bright, the leader of the Campus Crusade for Christ movement, when he says, "Though there are exceptions, God's communication to us in our day is seldom dramatic or unusual." [29] That statement does not, however, rule out the type of account I have just presented. It *does* mean that we should not be expecting such remarkable leadings in our own lives. Dr. Bright's advice is well stated: "Do not wait for God to speak to you in some dramatic way. Communion with Jesus Christ, obedience to His commands and trusting in His Spirit result in discovering God's will.''[30]

GOD LEADS BY DIFFICULT EXPERIENCES

No teenager has ever endured more heart-rending experiences or dramatic reverses than Joseph. He was the darling of his father. He lived in a fairly wealthy home. Everything was going so wonderfully for him until that traumatic day recorded in Genesis 37 when he was sent by his father to see how things were with his brothers in Dothan.

His brothers saw him coming and plotted to kill him. Reuben, one of those brothers, persuaded the rest of them not to kill him, but rather to put him down in a pit and let him die there. His intentions were good. He planned to rescue his brother later.

A caravan of Ishmaelites from Gilead came along on their way to Egypt. Joseph's brothers decided to sell him to them. He was carried off to a strange land, where there were strange gods, and strange customs. The culture shock, the hurt, the separations, the trauma, were almost unbearable. Yet those were only the beginnings of his troubles.

There in Egypt, Joseph was falsely accused of immorality, was put into prison, and was forgotten in that prison by Pharaoh's butler who promised to remember Joseph when he got out of prison. Yet *it was all in God's marvelous plan*! Through difficulties, God was preparing a mature man he could use to save many people, including his own family.

In Genesis 50:20 we read these thrilling words from the lips of Joseph to his assembled brothers: "You intended to harm me, but God intended it for good, to accomplish what is now being done, the saving of many lives." Joseph was not the last person who could testify that the hand of the Lord was in his reverses. The poet could say,

> Ill that He blesses is our good,
> And unblest good our ill,
> And all that seems most wrong is right,
> If it be His sweet will. [31]

And we can say that too!

I was presenting a series of practical messages in Aberdeen, South Dakota. A family, hurting badly because a son had been sent to prison, was very evidently on the heart of that congregation. Their one consolation was that the boy had made a new commitment of his life to Christ there in the penitentiary.

After one of the evening services, that dad and mother came to me with a joyful look on their faces, and handed a letter to me. It was a letter of encouragement their son had just received from a fellow Christian who had heard of his prison-made commitment to Christ. That gracious, thoughtful, encouraging letter was signed "Chuck Colson." Suddenly I remembered again that sometimes God leads us through the

39

difficult experiences of life. Chuck Colson's Prison Fellowship grew out of his own imprisonment for his part in Watergate.

Fran Reed of Anoka, Minnesota, has an effective ministry to people who are going through depression. As a missionary under the Latin American Mission in South America, both Bob and Fran had enjoyed fruitful ministries, but not particularly in the area of helping people who were distressed. Fran was an effervescent, always-on-top type of person. She could not empathize with those who were suffering from depression. They tried her patience. Why couldn't they just stop thinking about themselves and by sheer determination rise above their circumstances? *She* could!

Then followed the darkest valley of Fran's life. It seemed for a while as if there never would be light again. The depth of her depression was difficult for her to describe. During those days I told her many times that someday that trying experience would be used of the Lord for His glory in ministries she would have to others, but that I did not expect her to see that very clearly while feeling as she did.

When God brought her out of that valley of dark shadows it was into bright sunshine again, *and* into a new dimension of ministry—a ministry to others in their times of depression. The many months of nearly total darkness were in God's plan for her life.

Yes, God leads through difficult circumstances at times, and always so that He may enrich our lives and expand our usefulness.

40

GOD LEADS THROUGH
SPECIFIC INSTRUCTIONS

We all enjoy accounts of the dramatic, and the unusual. There is something in most of us that does not respond as readily to the regular diet upon which the Lord wants to feed us, however. But the clear instructions of His Word are to be our daily bread!

There are Christians who ask God for directions He has already given. The Bible is full of clear cut instructions as to how we are to live. We do not need to wonder whether or not we should read questionable books and articles in order to be well informed about the world around us and the society in which we live. Philippians 4:8 gives a clear answer to the issue of questionable reading materials. We are informed that the items we are to store in the data bank of our mind are the things that are true, noble, right, pure, lovely, admirable, and praiseworthy.

When I was a high school freshman, I asked my English teacher to recommend a good book for me to read. "I would like to recommend a book for you that is a little different from the ones you might usually read. It will help to broaden your life perspectives," she replied. She recommended *A Tree Grows in Brooklyn*. I checked the book out of the library and began to read it.

In the first chapter I found some things that offended my Christian sensitivity. I was startled, for Miss Higgins knew my testimony. It surprised me that she would recommend a book like that. I had confidence in her as a teacher, so I thought perhaps the book might get better in the second chapter. How naive! A book never starts out bad and gets better! Quite the opposite is true. I discovered that vividly in the second chapter.

Part of the way through that chapter I slammed the book closed. I took the book back to Miss Higgins, laid it on her desk and said, "Miss Higgins, you know I am a Christian. I do not intend to fill my mind with passionate scenes that can pollute my thought life in the days to come." With the book and the comment, I left this poem:

When you read, when you write
    When you seek for delight
When you walk, when you talk
    When you want to do right
To be kept from all wrong
    Both at home and abroad,
Live always as under
    The eyes of your God.

Whatever you sing in the midst of your glees,
    Sing nothing His listening ears would displease.
Whatever you say, in a whisper or clear,
    Say nothing you would not want Jesus to hear.
Whatever you read, though the page may allure,
    Read nothing of which you're not perfectly sure
Consternation at once would be seen in your look
    If God should say solemnly, 'Show *me* that

book!'
Wherever you go, never go where you fear
  Lest the great God should ask you,
  'How camest thou here?'
Turn away from each pleasure
  You'd shrink from pursuing
If God should look down and say,
  'What are you doing?' [32]

The section on reading I had underlined in red. There is no question as to whether or not God wants us to read sordid materials.

Neither is there any question as to whether or not a Christian should marry a non-Christian. "Do not be yoked together with unbelievers" is about as clear a statement from God as you could ask for. [33] In spite of this, I have known people to keep asking God for a clear answer. They ran from counselor to counselor hoping for some straw of encouragement they could clutch. Their hearts had become entangled, and they wanted God to make an exception for them, somehow.

One young lady came to me to ask how she could know the will of God in regard to a delightful young man with whom she had "fallen in love." He was not an unbeliever. As a matter of fact, he was a committed Christian and youth pastor of the church she attended. Their relationship, as she described it to me, had been characterized by spiritual desire and growth. They prayed together frequently. They had a mutual concern for souls. They both loved the Lord and now they had come to love each other deeply as well. I couldn't understand what her problem was. İt all sounded so delightful. If she loved him so much, and he loved her so much, and they wanted to serve the Lord together, why not? Then she told me. He was married! "But how could something so beautiful, and something that is causing such growth in my spiritual life be wrong?" she reasoned.

The heart is certainly deceitful above all things, just as the Bible claims.[34] There was no need to search for the will of God in this instance. God is as clear as crystal in His revealed Word as to how He feels about anything that would come between husband and wife. [35]

Many times through the years God has used Psalm 15:4b to help me know what He wants me to do. I cannot remember when I first discovered that verse. It may have been through my habit of reading the Bible through once each year, or it may have come from Paul Little's booklet on "Affirming the Will of God" which influenced my life greatly. I do know that it has had a big effect on me in helping me to stick by my promises. Psalm 15:4b states that God appreciates the person who does not go back on a promise simply because it does not turn out to be convenient.

Typical of the times when God has shown me His will through this verse was the occasion in Vancouver, British Columbia, when my wife, Elaine, and I had agreed to go to a lovely retirement lodge to conduct a church service following the evening service at our church. Shortly after that agreement had been made, my assistant pastor announced that there would be a

"Friendship In" following the service that very night. Friendship In was a very special night, delightfully planned, and always with delicious refreshments. This one was to be the once-a-year special when strawberry shortcake would be served. I knew that the strawberries would be picked the day before in the "U-Pick" fields of Richmond, and there are no better strawberries anywhere. I *love* strawberry shortcake! My first thought was, "Is there someone who could take our place at the Dogwood Lodge?" My second thought was from Psalm 15:4b. I knew immediately that there was no choice involved. We went to Dogwood Lodge (and back at church they saved us some strawberry shortcake!). God's clear Word was all that was needed.

Review with me the clear manner in which God has revealed portions of His will for you in the Bible: "The Lord is...not wanting anyone to perish, but everyone to come to repentance." [36] "It is God's will that you should be holy." [37] Clearly God is saying that He wills our salvation, He wills our holiness, and He wills as well our conformity "to the likeness of His son," the Lord Jesus Christ! [38] In multitudes of other areas He makes His will known and clear through Scripture.

GOD LEADS THROUGH SANCTIFIED REASON

Too often we are unwilling to trust our reasoning. We seem to feel it is not to be trusted. That idea needs to be questioned.

45

The apostles and elders met for discussion in Jerusalem. They needed to decide what to do with the new Gentile believers with regard to their obedience to Jewish laws and traditions. A lengthy discussion took place and when they had finished, James spoke up: "Brothers, listen to me...." He proceeded to make a brief speech and then said, "It is my judgment, therefore, that we should not make it difficult for the Gentiles who are turning to God. Instead we should...." and he went on to give the assembly his own judgment, which they promptly accepted. [39]

I am especially interested in the words of James, "It is my judgment." There are times when God expects us to use our own judgment after thinking things through carefully.

If my sons had come to me one Saturday while they were teenagers saying, "Dad, we have been invited to play basketball with some of the boys, but we have also been asked to go swimming with some others. Which would you prefer that we do?" I am sure I would have said, "It doesn't really matter to me. Do whatever you prefer."

Suppose Gary had countered with, "But Dad, we really want to know what you want us to do. We want to please you, and we will do which ever you tell us to do." I might have replied, "Well, frankly, either one would please me. They are both wholesome activities."

Brian might then have insisted, "Dad, you don't understand. We want to do *your* will, not our own. You tell us which we should do."

At this point I would have begun to get worried. There must be something wrong with these boys! They can't make a simple decision on their own. If they continued to press the issue, I would consider seeking psychological help for them!

We do that very thing with God. He has given us "sound minds" as Christians and He expects us to use those minds. M. Blaine Smith in his excellent book "Knowing God's Will" insists, "We should avoid the crystal ball approach to the Bible which looks for easy answers to difficult decisions and seeks to escape from our God-given responsibility for careful decision making."[40] So then, whether the decision is an easy one or a difficult one, we should use our sanctified reason as a major part of the decision making process. God is pleased to have it so.

When we are remaining in Christ and His words remain in us, we can ask the things *we* will, the Bible tells us![41] "Delight yourself in the Lord and he will give you the desires of *your* heart," God assures us through David.[42] In these two passages *our* will is emphasized. It is not in contradiction with the scripture that tells us that, "If we ask anything according to *His* will, he hears us."[43] When we are remaining in Him, abiding in Him, living in Him, *His* will becomes *our* will.

I stood in a mountain meadow in the moonlight with a six-foot-plus lumberjack in the shadow of the Yellowstone Mountains. He had asked if we might walk together following the evening service at Yellowstone Bible Camp near Bozeman, Montana. We talked about his longings after God's best in his life. At one memorable moment he lifted his towering head toward heaven, and with the moon's beams lighting the path of his tears down his cheeks and off the square edge of his chin, I heard him say so earnestly, "O God, I want what You want for my life. More than anything, *I want what You want!*" If you can say that with sincerity, then you can trust increasingly in your own judgment, for your reasonings become more and more divinely led.

There are times when we are forced to make our own decision without some special direction from heaven. That should not unduly distress us. If God does not speak in some clearly discernible manner, we should use our own best judgment, after having had prayer for wisdom.

I agree whole-heartedly with Margaret Erb in her essay "God Has a Plan" when she says, "Occasionally there is a time element in making a decision, and we do not sense God's will in the matter before we must make a choice. In that case we must carefully consider all the facts and, using our God-given brains, make the best judgment we can—trusting Him to protect us from a wrong decision." [44]

GOD LEADS THROUGH THE COUNSEL OF GODLY PEOPLE

Fellow Christians cannot be expected to make your decisions for you, but they certainly can be used of God to confirm His plans for your life. Be careful which fellow Christians you turn to, however. I like the qualifications Paul Little attaches to the idea of consulting with Christian friends. He says, "God guides us through the counsel of other Christians who are fully committed to the will of God and who know us well."[45] Godly people who are committed to the will of God themselves often have a degree of discernment that is very beneficial to us if we are wise enough to utilize it. They *do* need to know us well, for this aids them in their judgment.

Beware of the decision that is questioned by other Christians whom you hold in high regard. Inward pain is inevitable when I think of a choice teenage girl in one of our pastorates. We all knew and loved her for her continual smile, her depth of commitment to the Lord Jesus, and her zeal to share her faith with others. She became fully convinced that God wanted her to marry a man newly come to Christ, and serving a prison term of considerable duration.

She consulted with many godly persons for whom she had much respect. Every one of them thought her decision premature and unwise. She went from one to another until finally, unable to find the confirmation she wanted, she turned from them all to pursue her own way.

Never, never trust inner convictions that godly people who know you well cannot affirm.

The consensus of the conference at Jerusalem to which we referred earlier was summarized in a letter to the Gentiles. In that letter the leaders stated, "It seemed good to the Holy Spirit and *to us*...."[46] If your decision is in the will of God, it should be prompted by the Holy Spirit and confirmed by godly people who know you well.

GOD LEADS THROUGH
DEVOTIONAL APPLICATION

One of the most frequent ways by which God speaks to His people is through Bible reading in the course of their daily devotions.

If any controversial element exists among these avenues to determining God's will that I am suggesting, it is to be found in this subjective approach to the reading of the Bible.

Please be careful to note that for decision-making this method should be used only in conjunction with other methods. Too great a reliance upon *any* one approach, in fact, can result in well-meaning error, and even in ultimate confusion.

To the person who has been a recipient of God's intimate and personal leading through His Word, there is no need for lengthy attempts at justification of such subjectivity.

To the unthinking, who have a tendency to "latch onto" a Scripture text, and base a decision upon a very subjective application of it without testing the validity of that application, I would give a firm word of caution. It is this: God's leadings *must* and *will* stand the test of cross-checking with various means of guidance.

To the rigid who would allow only for an intellectual, objective approach in their Bible reading, with all the rules of proper hermeneutical treatment unswervingly applied, I would give a reminder of the living nature of the Scriptures. [47]

The Bible is far more than an historical

document. It would long since have had to relinquish its best seller status were it not for its genius as a living, life-giving creation of God Himself. To call it a "book" in the ordinary sense of the word, is demeaning. The Bible has life that has been breathed into it divinely. It functions in a creative manner that sets it apart from all other books.

I again urge you not to miss the point that such a subjective approach to your Bible reading as I am here proposing *is valid in conjunction with other methods* of discerning the will of God.

Don't miss the thrill of hearing the voice of God to your own soul because you are afraid of subjectivity. Objectivity is important, certainly, but a mingling of subjectivity and objectivity may add a dimension of delight and reality to your devotions and to your Christian experience that you have previously missed.

While pastoring on Long Island in New York State, Elaine and I felt that there was a great need for an evangelical church in Commack, Long Island. It was a community that would grow from 350 people to 35,000 people in just ten years! Homes were springing up like mushrooms from what were formerly potato fields. There was not one evangelical church in that exploding community.

We thought it would be wise to sponsor a Bible college student to serve there, letting our church in West Hempstead, Long Island, be the "mother" church. I could not get away from a growing feeling, however, that perhaps we should go there ourselves. A person with

51

ministerial experience might be more effective than someone newly trained and without that experience.

Our reasoning against the idea ran like this: "Lord, we would enjoy doing something like that, but you know that our denomination has no funds with which to back another extension church right now. If we were to go without a few meals, it would be no disaster. We could fast and pray! We do have a baby, though, and the baby wouldn't understand missing even one meal! It seems more logical to send a single student there, with a little less financial responsibility."

Immediately after such reasoning and prayer, I opened my Bible where the bookmark was (my pattern is to read from Genesis to Revelation regularly). The scripture for that very morning included the text, "So shalt *thou* dwell in the land, and *verily thou shalt be fed.*" [48] I was deeply touched, and bowed my head before reading another verse. In continuation of the dialog, I prayed, "Lord, that's so clear, so very clear, but still I question the 'How' of it all. The mansion we want to buy is so expensive. The other prospective buyer (a man notorious for his immorality) has $80,000 cash to offer, and we have only $27 in the bank at this point!"

I went on with my reading and in the sixteenth verse of that same Psalm I was amazed to hear God say, "A little that a righteous man hath is better than the riches of many wicked." [49] Before I left the devotional time that morning, I knew that Elaine and I were the ones who would be opening The Neighborhood Church of Commack,

Long Island. And open it we did! God's hand of blessing was upon that work in ways that greatly glorified His own name.

I believe that God delights to reveal His will to us through our devotional reading. Be very careful, however, that you do not read looking for something that will support your own thinking. This is the reason that during times of searching for specific guidance in an important matter I set a specific number of chapters and read no more and no less than that specified number. God *must* speak to me through those chapters, or not at all through His Word. I am very conscious of the fact that if I read long enough looking for something to support what I want to do, I will probably find it, and that is dangerous.

Elaine and I made a trip to a city where a strong, aggressive church was asking us to candidate. We were quite willing to stay where we were, but felt we had to explore this particular invitation. When we arrived in the city, we found an alive group of people, with wonderful plans, but a depressingly deteriorated building in a terribly unclean city with a drab and unappealing climate.

We desperately wanted to do the will of God, but did not find it in our hearts to be excited about ministering in such a place. Sitting in the motel one morning, Elaine saw me pick up my Bible for devotions, and knowing how God speaks to me through His Word, she blurted out, "Oh honey, find something that says 'Go back!' " I laughed (with mixed emotions struggling within me) and said, "Honey, we don't look for what *we* want Him to say!'' ''Oh, I know that,'' she said. And of course she did! Elaine is as committed to the will of God as I am. She was just being honest with me about her feelings (and reflecting my unexpressed ones, as well!).

I opened my Bible where the bookmark was, and to my amazement, the very first verse for that morning's reading was, ''David then asked the Lord, 'Shall I move back to Judah?' And the Lord replied, 'Yes.' ''[50] We knew immediately that God was releasing us from this possibility of service. Further confirmations came to affirm that release. Note: I am not reluctant to ask God to reconfirm, even when He has spoken clearly. I feel motivation makes the difference when asking for confirmations.

I wish to give a word of caution. In order for you to be confident of God's instructions coming to you in this manner, you need to be consistent in your devotional reading, not haphazard. There needs to be a feeling that those chapters are God's chapters for you for that morning. An impression like that arises out of a regular pattern of reading.

Section III of this book will vividly illustrate God's use of ''devotional application'' as a method of revealing His will to us. He has used it literally dozens of times in my life, and it is a temptation for me to forget that God deals with each of us in His own chosen ways. His pattern of dealing with you may be quite different from His pattern of dealing with me. I still believe that devotional application is one of God's major ways of leading His people, since it honors His Word, and encourages faithful Bible reading.

GOD LEADS BY OPEN DOORS

Open doors as well as shut doors are mentioned pointedly in God's Word. "What he opens, no one can shut; and what he shuts, no one can open....See, I have placed before you an open door that no one can shut," God said to the church in Philadelphia. [51]

Paul wrote to the Corinthians, "...a great door for effective work has opened to me." [52] I relate to Paul's statement, for looking back over my life I can thoughtfully state that almost every major decision of my life came about through the opening of some door to me, and then the confirmation from God that this open door was one through which He would have me walk. Open doors need to be prayerfully considered, usually.

While open doors are not necessarily God's invitation to walk through them, there is always that possibility. I have been cautious about pushing a door open. I want God to know that I am fully committed to walking through the doors He opens, leaving politicking and maneuvering behind.

That is not to say that we should fail to prepare ourselves for the fulfillment of our heart's desires. God has "prepared places for prepared people." [53] It *is* to say that the door of opportunity is best opened by God Himself and not by man. I plan to relate a vivid illustration of

55

this in Section III. When we have thoroughly prepared ourselves for something we would like to do, and God has added His own special training and enabling, the opening of a door becomes an exciting climax, if He has opened it!

GOD LEADS THROUGH THE GIVING OF AN INNER PEACE

Conflicting statements are made by equally sincere Christian writers as to whether God leads by an inner conviction or peace. Oliver R. Barclay, in his book *Guidance*, contends rather strongly that "...he has never promised to lead us by inward convictions but only by wisdom, judgment and advice based upon knowledge of and obedience to Scriptures."[54]

While it may be true that He has not promised such an inward conviction or peace, it is undeniably true that multitudes of Christians can testify to inner peace coming to them as a sweet aspect of their decision-making when those decisions have been in the will of God.

Margaret Erb, in her essay "God Has a Plan," testifies, "Personally I have found that I have a sense of peace and happiness in my heart when I have made the right decision. Conversely, if the decision is not according to God's will I have an unsettled feeling, a restlessness, which causes me to re-think and re-pray the whole matter."[55]

She also testifies, "From personal experience I know that when I am in close fellowship with God there is a wonderful way in which His Spirit

56

speaks to my spirit in matters where I need His guidance.''[56] This is a very subjective aspect of knowing the will of God. We need a balance and probably a combination of factors in ascertaining God's will, but I will not rule out the ''inner peace'' factor, for to me (and I think to most of us) it is an important factor.

The lack of peace so evident in the prophet Elijah when he was out of the will of God while fleeing from Jezebel is significant here. ''I've had enough! Let me die,'' was his heartcry while there in his deep depression. By contrast, the peace that passes understanding is illustrated vividly by Paul and Silas in the prison with their hands and feet fast in the stocks, their mouths dry, their backs bleeding, and yet they are *singing* at midnight! They were in the will of God and they knew it, and their inner peace could not be touched by their outer circumstances.

When your final decision is made, there should be a substantial measure of inner peace that accompanies it, or it might be well for you to reevaluate that decision.

GOD LEADS IN A GREAT VARIETY OF WAYS

In no way do I mean to imply that this listing of the ways by which the Lord leads is an exhaustive or complete list. To restrict God to such a list would be to limit His exciting personality which is characterized by an infinite variety. The God who made each snowflake different from all others cannot be squeezed into a restrictive mold fashioned by man.

Without dictating the means by which God should speak, our great heartcry ought to be, "Lord, speak to me that I may speak in living echoes of Thy tone!"[57] The life that is led by God Himself reflects the glory of a living God who is wonderfully active and current and contemporary.

Section III

GOD'S WILL
How Personal is It?

The decade of 1960 to 1970—that was an exciting time for me! Teaching in a Bible college was *multiplication*. Earlier years in the pastorate had been *addition*. The young men and women in my classes would be scattered all over the world someday sharing Christ (today they are, hundreds of them). All my life I would thrill over their accomplishments, the way a parent does over the achievements of his own children.

But there was a fly in the ointment. A few of our finest students at the St. Paul Bible College hit snags in their initial assignments after graduation. "Snag" is not a strong enough word for it. Sometimes it seemed like a *brick wall* to them. I received letters, sometimes from distant places, pouring out deep frustration, expressing the longing for growth and blessing in their churches, smarting over lack of cooperation, reaching out for help. I answered those letters faithfully and promptly, but sometimes that was not sufficient. One exceptionally keen young man I had helped to train left the ministry to sell automobiles. Another one quit the pastorate to write income tax forms for H & R Block. Some of those young pastors in difficulty weathered their storms successfully, but for a while they endured the pain of feeling almost forsaken—*even by God Himself!*

"Lord, someday...someday let me establish a retreat center to which Christian workers can come in their times of frustration, weariness, decision-making. Let it be a place where there is quietness and rest for all who come, and where I can offer daily counseling to those who want it. Let it be a place where there are no telephones, no schedules and no pressures. Let it be a place where a person can renew his strength and get things back into perspective."

The dream was born (born of God, I believe!).

Those years at the St. Paul Bible College were busy ones. Included in my regular schedule were courses at the university to further my education. Most of those courses were in guidance and counseling. They would equip me better for my position as Dean of Students at the college, and would also prepare me for a counseling ministry at the retreat center someday.

The decision to leave St. Paul Bible College in 1970 to pastor a small, new church in Anoka, Minnesota, followed the usual pattern of God's leading in my life. Through my daily Bible reading God gave me scriptures that clearly indicated that this was His plan for us.

The next eight years proved decisively that my return to the pastorate certainly *was* God's plan. The church broke ground for new facilities almost every one of those eight years. Attendance rose into the hundreds. Land acquisition totalled 55 acres to serve as a campus for the growing church and for the new Christian school. Meadow Creek Christian School was established in 1975 and five years later was training over three hundred students. The giving to worldwide missions rose to nearly $100,000 a year. It was a delightful assignment! When God would be ready to move us, He would need to make it *very* clear!

During those years in Anoka, I made a trip into the Appalachian Mountains of Tennessee. My purpose was to find another outlet for the expanding missionary giving of our independent church. However, that trip was to have profound significance in another direction.

In the course of my trip, I stopped at Moody Aviation in Elizabethton, Tennessee. Standing by the fence near the runway there, I noted the beauty of the surrounding mountains, the peacefulness of the valley, and the semi-isolation of the area. The thought came to me forcefully that it would be a good place to establish that retreat center I had dreamed about. Perhaps right up there on the slopes of that mountain on the other side of the runway would be a good spot.

It would be a thrill to be able to look down from those heights and see planes taking off and landing. They would be continual reminders of total commitment. The young pilots were preparing for missionary service, knowing well the hazards of such service in rugged terrain.

"Lord, let us have 25 acres right up there on

the slopes of that mountain," I prayed. I added that request to my prayer list and brought it before God regularly in the years that followed.

Invitations to candidate had come to us from time to time during those eight years in Anoka. It had always been easy to turn them down with a brief expression of appreciation for the church's interest. Two new invitations, however, could not be so lightly dismissed. I did not feel the freedom to say a quick "no" to them. Akron, Ohio, was the source of one of those invitations. "Dear Lord, we need wisdom. Are we to remain here in Anoka? Are you moving us to Akron? What is Your will in this matter?"

As usual, I set a number of chapters per day for my devotional reading during this time of searching. I expected God to speak through those chapters, if He chose to speak to us through Scripture.

While in Akron, one of the board members of the church gave us a tour of the city. We saw the famous Cathedral of Tomorrow, the huge tire factories, and the new property on which the church people planned to break ground within weeks. The candidating experience was delightful. That large group of consecrated men along with their dedicated wives took us to the Cathedral Buffet, a lavish smorgasbord. It was an experience in fellowship and food we would not soon forget. They were excited about their plans to build on eleven acres of ground they had acquired just on the other side of the expressway. Their relocation program would take them from the inner city and an old building to a newer area and a brand new octagonal auditorium with marvelous educational facilities. Their excitement was contagious. The question: Was God asking us to lead them in this bold, new venture of faith? The unanimous call they extended was not sufficient—we needed to hear from God Himself.

The plane left Akron so early that Monday morning that I did not have time to have my devotions in Ohio. I would do so in Minnesota upon arriving home. Just before sitting down with my Bible, I browsed through the pile of mail. I noticed among the letters one from a Canadian District Superintendent, Roy McIntyre, inviting us to candidate in the well known Tenth Avenue Alliance Church in Vancouver, British Columbia! I had often heard of that great church, and knew as well something of the beauty of that area with its majestic mountains, its blue waters, and its strikingly beautiful harbor; I also knew that we did not make our decisions on the basis of blue water, tall mountains, parks, and harbors!

I picked up my Bible to read. Before opening where the bookmark was, I prayed, "Lord, what could you say this morning that would point us either toward Akron, or toward Vancouver? I cannot imagine, but I ask you to speak."

In the course of my reading the specified number of chapters for that morning, I came to a verse which read, "Rabbah..." (Now, what do you know about Rabbah? Probably as much as I did—nothing! I had read my Bible through nineteen times, but I couldn't tell you one thing about Rabbah!) "...Rabbah and its beautiful harbor are ours."[58]

While I knew nothing about Rabbah, I certainly was aware of the legendary beauty of the harbor in Vancouver, set like a deep blue jewel between the majestic mountains on the north and the towering skyscrapers on the south, and flanked by Stanley Park on the west and Burrard Inlet and Deep Cove on the east. In my heart I felt we would be going to Vancouver. Only time would tell. God would have to confirm again and again His directions, to make the way crystal clear.

Vancouver was all we had expected and more. Queen Elizabeth Park on "Little Mountain" was natural beauty groomed to perfection. The profusion of flowers and flowering shrubs and trees, the picturesque beauty of marinas and of sailboats with their billowing, colorful spinnakers, all mingled into a panorama of unparalleled magnificance. We had never "oohed" and "aahed" so much in any place, not even Hong Kong!

The church people were warm and enjoyable. The board was most gracious. The large buildings were located in the inner city and, according to the annual reports, numerical decline had characterized the previous twelve years. In spite of the decline, it was still a strong church of nearly six hundred, and they possessed the numerical and financial strength to make the move to the suburbs.

When I discovered that a recent board decision had been made to remain on that inner city corner and not to move, I made it very clear to the board that I was not the man they were looking for. If they had been led of God in this decision, I told them, and were willing to give of themselves without reservations to the monumental task before them, more power to them! It would take a miracle from heaven for a middle class group of people to bridge the great cultural gap that existed between them and the people who surrounded the church. "If God is in this decision," I said, "may He also enable with the needed miracle."

My philosophy ran cross-grain to that of the board, and when Elaine and I left Vancouver, we never expected to hear from them again. One of the greatest surprises of my life came when Roy McIntyre phoned a few days later. He said, "The men in Vancouver are in session right now. They have just completed a secret ballot. The vote was 32 'yes' and not a single 'no.' They are asking you to come as the pastor of their church, and they want me especially to tell you that the vote included the program you outlined, including relocation as the Lord enables. They are completely reversing themselves and they want to stand 100 percent behind you."

Elaine and I were stunned! It seemed like a miracle. "Lord Jesus, we are willing to go, but you must confirm this—it is such a big move!"

The next day in my devotions, where the bookmark was, I read, "The God of Heaven has now given me the responsibility of building Him a temple." [59] Those words had never had such great significance for me before!

The following day before picking up my Bible I prayed, "Lord, we are willing to go and undertake this staggering assignment, but the finances scare me. The land that would be available within the area the board members would consider a reasonable distance to move is selling for nearly $250,000 an acre. Land alone could run as much as $2 million before we even dig a hole!" I opened where my bookmark was and began to read. "If you run short of money for the construction of the temple...you may requisition funds from the royal treasury."[60]

I am not given to shouting, but a strong "hallelujah" escaped my lips at that moment!

By devotional application God was leading us to Vancouver. A total of nineteen verses were used by God to confirm and reconfirm this appointment, and we went to Vancouver knowing surely that we were following God's directions and not merely man's invitation.

While in Vancouver, we worked diligently to explore every possible site for the new "temple." In "beautiful British Columbia" (as it is frequently called) we wanted to erect a strikingly beautiful edifice in which a beautiful Jesus would be proclaimed. There was no way I could have realized how short-lived our ministry would be among those people we came to love so dearly, and in what is unquestionably one of the most beautiful spots on God's earth.

There were many obstacles to the building of a new church in Vancouver. Land was exceedingly scarce. An exciting lead had some of us concocting vivid imaginations. Eleven acres of land that were being used as a golf driving range came up for sale. The land was situated right on the busy Trans Canada Highway at an important interchange in a better than average section of the city. The criteria we had established for a future location were all converging on that piece of land. It had (1) visibility, (2) centrality, (3) accessibility, (4) usability (by which we meant six or more acres). It was all there!

There were three prospective buyers in line ahead of us. Two of them backed out or were unable to secure financing. It came right down to the last one ahead of us, and then our dreams fell through. That choice location was sold to the group representing our last obstacle.

The massive amount of research that had to be done was handed over to a consulting firm. A very large evangelical Chinese church showed strong interest in purchasing the Tenth Avenue facilities.

Yet in spite of all of this, precious months were slipping away. People in sizable numbers were moving to the suburbs. The ground work for relocation was proceeding too slowly to suit my gung-ho spirit. There was certainly progress, and I was determined not to lose faith in the directions God had given to us. God had brought us to Vancouver for a specific purpose, and we would do all within our power to obey His orders.

Elaine and our younger son, Gary, were sitting at the kitchen table with me one day when they brought up a concern of theirs. They had noticed that I was talking more and more about "Fairhaven Ministries," the name I had now given to my dream of a retreat center in Elizabethton, Tennessee. They were puzzled as to how my increasingly frequent references to Fairhaven fit in with the assignment God had given to build a "temple" in Vancouver. I really had no answer to this observation. But it did make me think!

It was true that I was doing a lot of daydreaming about Fairhaven. I had even drawn a diagram of how we would put roads up the mountain on those 25 acres I was praying for above the runway. I had spotted the lodge and the individual chalets on that fanciful "map." I had picked "out of the blue" the name "Fairhaven Ministries" because it seemed to say what I wanted it to say about the place. (Later I would realize that it had indeed come "out of the blue" but in no arbitrary fashion, as I then thought!)

Elaine's and Gary's thoughtful question caused me to give myself with more diligence to the planning of the new church building in Vancouver. I tried not to talk about Fairhaven... but I couldn't stop my mind from thinking about it. It became almost an obsession!

One day I said to Elaine and Gary, "I am going to change my way of praying. Instead of praying that we will be able to buy 25 acres there on the mountain in Elizabethton along about 1985, I am going to pray that when God's own time comes for the establishing of Fairhaven Ministries, He will have a lodge, or a chalet, or a resort already built and ready for use. That would mean that we could immediately begin to have guests instead of going down there and acquiring 25 acres, and then taking a year or more to develop it before we could have any guests."

I prayed that way seven days. On the seventh day one of my secretaries came into my office and said, "There is a long distance phone call for you on line one." I picked up the phone to answer. The male voice on the other end said, "Hello, Chuck. Remember me? My name's Clyde Powell."

"No, Clyde, I'm sorry, your name is familiar, but I can't place you, except that I know you are from my Nyack College days. That's the only place I was ever called Chuck."

"That's no problem," he continued, "I just called to tell you that I have heard about your dream."

"What dream?" I countered (my mind would not get into gear).

"Your dream of a place for Christian workers to come to in their crisis times. I wanted you to know that God gave us a similar dream a couple of years ago. We left our place of employment and moved into the mountains to build a chalet. It's nearly finished. It has four separate units, each with private entrance. They are fully carpeted. Each has its own kitchen, fully equipped. Each has a buck stove fireplace. They have balconies that hang out toward a trout stream. It's modern and beautiful and will be ready for use June 1. Can you come to begin your ministry then?"

"No way—no way!" I answered. "God brought us here to build a new church in Vancouver and we are far from accomplishing that assignment." The incongruity of praying that God would have a chalet already built as an indication of *His* timing, and then saying *"no way"* when the prayer was answered did not cross my mind at that moment.

"That's okay, we'll just rent to Moody students while we are waiting for you to come," Clyde said.

"Moody students! Where are you located, Clyde?"

"Near Elizabethton, Tennessee," he responded.

I was so overwhelmed I couldn't speak again until I regained control of my emotions. Elizabethton was the very geographical pinpoint on the North American continent I had chosen for Fairhaven, and he was telling me that he had built the chalet near there!

The days that followed that phone call were characterized by confusion. On the one hand there was the thrill of realizing that God had so remarkably answered a seven-day prayer. I had to feel that it was most likely not my prayer at all, but a God-inspired one! On the other hand, there was the puzzlement of realizing that the church had not been built in Vancouver as promised so specifically before we went there. God had clearly given us a Vancouver assignment, and now He appeared to be issuing new marching orders. How could that be? How could I trust what I considered to be His leading, if somehow I had made a mistake two years before when we came to Vancouver following what we thought was His leading? How could we synthesize these conflicting cues?

I made an appointment with my new district superintendent, Gordon Fowler. I respected him very highly and knew he would listen to me and try to help me. "How do I put this all together?" I asked. "I really don't know," he answered honestly. I didn't really expect him to know, down deep in my heart, but it was good to have him listen to me and pray for me.

As he was praying, suddenly there forced its way into my mind a passage of Scripture I had never memorized. It really isn't the kind of passage you tend to memorize! It said something to the effect that the prophet who had given David the blessing to go ahead with the building of the temple was sent back to him again with the words, "You are not the one to build my temple." So forceful was that impression that I told Gordon about it when he finished praying.

When I got back home I told Elaine about it as well, adding the words, "If those verses would come in tomorrow morning's devotions, I would know they were from God. But the trouble is that I'm not reading about David just now."

That evening Elaine and Gary asked me if I would like to play a game with them. We are great game-players at our house. I demurred, saying that I had something else I wanted to do. I didn't tell them that I wanted to have tomorrow morning's devotions ahead of time! I've never done that in all my life, before nor since, but I just couldn't wait to see what the Lord might say.

I opened my New International Version Bible where the bookmark was. That version has paragraph headings in it, and the first thing I saw when I cracked the book was, "David Becomes King Over Israel."[61] Almost immediately I knew what I would find in that day's devotions.

I was reading twelve pages a day during those days of seeking for the will of God in this matter, and after reading seven pages the remembered passage had not appeared. I began to wonder whether it would be found in that day's reading or not. If God were going to confirm what seemed to be His call, He would have to do it within the confines of those twelve pages. My rule is adamant—not to frustrate God, but to be certain in my own soul that it really comes from God.

On the eighth page of reading, I felt a leap of joy within my heart as I came to the passage:

That night the word of God came to Nathan, saying:

"Go and tell my servant David, 'This is what the Lord says: You are not the one to build me a house to dwell in....I have been with you wherever you have gone....I declare to you that the Lord will build a house....' "[62]

David's response to this word from God suited so perfectly the feelings of my own heart.

Then King David went in and sat before the Lord, and he said:

"Who am I, O Lord God, and what is my family, that you have brought me this far?"[63]

"What more can David say to you...you know your servant, O Lord, and according to your will, you have done this great thing and made known all these great

promises. There is none like you, O
Lord...."[64]

I was so overcome with this specific word from
heaven, found right where my bookmark was for
that day's reading, that I cried for joy. How near,
and how dear our Lord is! With tears, I shared
this with Elaine and Gary.

The next two days God reconfirmed those
words! On the second day I read:

> David said to Solomon, "My son, I had it
> in my heart to build a house for the Name
> of the Lord my God. But this word of the
> Lord came to me:...You are not to build a
> house for my Name."[65]

On the third day I read:

> My father David had it in his heart to build
> a temple for the Name of the Lord, the
> God of Israel. But the Lord said to my
> father David, "Because it was in your
> heart to build a temple for my Name, you
> did well to have this in your heart.
> Nevertheless, you are not the one to build
> the temple..."[66]

There was no mistaking the fact that the God
who had sent us to Vancouver, using nineteen
verses of specific instructions, was now giving
new orders. It was a definite change of direction,
and I felt as certain of it as King David did of his
new instructions contradicting the old ones. I
knew God had released us from Vancouver and
reassigned us to Tennessee.

"Dear Lord, we need confirmation! This is a
huge move. It would be the greatest step of faith
we have ever taken. We must have You confirm

75

it all along the way. There is no Fairhaven Ministries asking us to come and be the director. It is all a burning vision, but with no more substance than a vision except as You put it all together. *We need confirmation!"*

I wrote to fourteen district superintendents who were acquaintances or personal friends. I spelled out for them what we wanted to do, and then asked pointed questions: "Do you see a need for a place like this?" "If there were such a place, would you refer your men there?" "Looking back over the years, do you feel you would have used such a facility once a year for your workers? Less? More?" To these specific questions came back specific answers. All fourteen experienced men were enthusiastic.

From Nebraska came a reply:

An excellent idea! I believe with all my heart that there is a great need for a place of retreat and renewal. For the record, I would like to indicate my hearty approval of the plan. I would estimate that we would use it at least twice a year. This is a much needed facility. [67]

Another reply arrived from Wheaton, Illinois:

My immediate response is a very positive one. I have sensed great need along this line, and can see where such a program would have great value in the restoring of some who, because of circumstances, have reached a point of discouragement, or weariness, or defeat, or confusion. Right now I would have as many as three men I would like to recommend to such a service. [68]

From central Canada came the reply:

This is a very important area that we need to address our attention to. I am finding that more pastors are hurting today than ever before. There is a whole new attitude developing in our churches that gives me a great deal of concern. People seem to be very demanding and at the same time, not very considerate or patient with their pastoral leadership. In my role as District Superintendent I am also coming to a realization that many pastors and their wives are having serious conflict in their marriage relationship. Seldom does this come to the surface until it is almost too late to save the ministry of the couple. [69]

These and other letters confirmed the need beyond question.

I wrote to Bill Nabors, the District Superintendent for The Christian and Missionary Alliance in the Southern District, to tell him of my dream and of the possibility of its fulfillment within his district. My question to him was whether or not the credentials I had held with The Christian and Missionary Alliance for thirty years could be continued, since I would be serving in an independent organization, not affiliated with any denomination. We would be serving Christian workers from any denominational or non-denominational background.

He picked up his phone and called me across three thousand miles! "Of course we will credential you in our district. We are pleased to have this happening within our borders, and will do everything we can to back you. Let's meet at the General Council in Lincoln and talk about it." I was so pleased by his graciousness.

At the General Council of The Christian and Missionary Alliance, delegates, corresponding delegates, and visitors numbered into the thousands. Looking for Bill Nabors was like hunting for a needle in a haystack, especially when I couldn't remember what he looked like. Dark hair, medium build, and rather nice looks were more frequent than I had realized before!

Each query to someone I thought might know him brought a response of this sort: "Well, he was right over there a minute ago, but I don't see him just now." The frustration mounted as the week slipped away, and by the last full day of Council, I was getting anxious.

Then I noticed that Mr. Nabors's name was listed among the 60 communion stewards for serving communion in that thrilling Saturday morning service. "Lord Jesus, You could bring Mr. Nabors to *our* row, if You wish. Would it please You to do that?"

Name tags are removed when the men serve communion, and I didn't know the men serving near us. Norman Valentine, a very special friend, was sitting beside me. "Ned, do you see Mr. Nabors anywhere?" Ned raised his finger in a sharp angle up to the left, and I saw it was pointing to the man who was serving *our* row! One out of 60! There were 59 other places in that huge auditorium to which he could have been assigned. "Thank you, Lord Jesus." It was a *very* special communion service!

"Lord Jesus, I would like to talk to Dr. Keith Bailey, if it would please You. I know there are many things to militate against that possibility, but You are able to arrange it."

The request was a big one (to my way of thinking). Dr. Bailey is well known. In the crowd that mills around the hotel lobbies, the meeting rooms, and the booths at General Council, it is almost impossible without prior arrangement to have a half hour with someone as important as he.

Dr. Bailey had been the chief administrator, under the president of the denomination, over all the district superintendents and pastors in North America. His years of experience would make him a choice person to respond to my idea-dream. God could arrange it, but would He please to?

I came down from our room in the Clayton House, surprised to note that there was not another person on that elevator. That seldom happens in one of the major Council hotels. The situation in the lobby was an even greater surprise. There was not one person to be seen with the exception of Dr. Keith Bailey. He was sitting alone, looking out of the large plate glass windows as if waiting for someone.

"Dr. Bailey, may I speak to you for a while?" I asked. "Of course," he responded in his characteristically pleasant manner. "I am expecting my son to come to pick me up at any moment, but we may talk until he arrives," he said.

I shared my dream with him. I asked for his

reactions based upon his years of experience.

"Get on with your idea as soon as you can," he urged. "The need is far greater than you realize. The pressures of society and of the pastorate in this day of rapid change are increasingly heavy. We are finding that there are more drop-outs and more discipline problems than ever before."

Here was someone who knew the field thoroughly, and he was telling me that the need was greater than I had dreamed!

"This is all very exciting," Elaine said one day, "but where will our food come from? And what about our boys? We have always planned to stand behind them financially during their years of preparation for whatever the Lord would have them do. Brian is training at Moody Aviation and Gary is leaving for the St. Paul Bible College this fall. How are we going to manage financially?"

She wasn't trying to put a wet blanket on a delightful fire. Elaine is just what I need when my dreaming spirit soars. I have a tendency to ignore the practical side of things with unstudied ease!"Honey, the Lord will take care of all of those things," I answered with conviction. In my mind, however, I added to her two concerns my own thoughts of our dream of laying aside an inheritance for the boys. If they should spend their lives in Christian service on a subsistence allowance, we had wanted to be able to leave them a comfortable inheritance on which they could rely for retirement years.

The next morning, before opening my Bible where the bookmark was, I prayed, "Dear Lord, reassure me that You *will* take care of every need, even to answering our prayer that Brian may graduate from Moody Aviation debt free. Show me from Your Word this morning.''

My bookmark was located in the early part of the book of Psalms. I opened my Bible and read, ''You still the hunger of those you cherish; their sons have plenty, and they store up wealth for their children.''[70] God had addressed Himself to the three areas of concern, and I didn't even know there was such a verse in the Bible! It is wonderfully strange how we can read the Bible many times and not see in it what suddenly becomes a direct word from heaven to our hearts. Current circumstance, and God's sweet timing, make the difference. That's part of the genius of the living Word and of our living God. He *enjoys* speaking to us like that, I believe.

We made a trip to Tennessee following Council in Lincoln, Nebraska. We needed to meet Clyde and Marguerite Powell, the builders of the chalet. We needed to see it all for ourselves, and have another confirmation in our spirits that this was the will of God through sensing that they were the kind of people with whom we could work in harmony. Staff harmony would be so tremendously important in a retreat center such as we envisioned.

The chalet was more than we had dreamed of! Nestled in a ravine beside Tiger Creek near Roan Mountain, Tennessee, it was a bit of Switzerland imported to the Smokies. We were delighted! The tastefully decorated units were warm and inviting. We could imagine our guests being excited and encouraged when first walking into

81

such beautiful surroundings.

More important than that were our impressions of Clyde and Marguerite. Immediately we felt a bond of fellowship. The warmth of their love which we experienced would also enfold many, many guests in future days, if God were to continue to bring all this together.

Clyde had a twinkle in his dark eyes that spoke of sanctified mischief! Marguerite was vivacious and a picturesque package of concentrated energy in her coveralls and rakish tam as she swung her weedcutter on the slopes of the seventeen acre site.

Laughter and fellowship and progressive thinking were only a few of the ingredients that made those happy days at the chalet so memorable. We *knew* we would have no difficulty working with people like these former missionaries to Viet Nam. Long since they had learned the joy of getting along with others, and the fulfillment of living for others. Their sincere walk with God would be a resource upon which our guests could draw in the days ahead.

We could see God's hand so clearly at work during those days. One morning I contacted Carl McCutcheon, a local realtor who was very highly recommended to us by a Moody Aviation student. I liked Carl immediately. The pipe he carried in his hand struck me as incongruous with the youthful look on his face. His mustache helped to modify that impression. He was disarmingly soft-spoken and was characterized by a studied approach to things, but in no way did it grow out of lack of expertise. He was a most capable and open-hearted person. Our friendship grew rapidly.

His wife, Lori, was a petite, fun-loving blonde who decorated and maintained her home and her family's appearance with great care. We learned that her cooking skills were finely honed as well when Carl and Lori invited us to their attractive brick home with its commanding view of the foothills of the Smokies. I had the great joy of eventually pointing them both to Christ.

"Carl, what do you have in the way of acreages?" I asked. "I have six acres down on Gap Creek Road," he replied. "No, I'm thinking of a lot more acres than that, Carl. We are planning a retreat center that will expand considerably from its small beginnings." "Well, I have one other piece," he said. "It is fifty acres in size and is located up on the mountain behind Moody Aviation."

Before even seeing that parcel of land, I knew in my heart that it was the answer to my prayer of many years for a 25 acre tract up there on that mountain. God was giving us twice the acreage I had asked Him for, right where I had requested it. Could it be that once again we were witnessing God's plan unfolding, with our own part in it being divinely prompted, so as to bring maximum glory to Himself? I sincerely believed so.

The story of the acquiring of the land belongs in another place. It is enough here to say that the vistas from the various plateaus on those fifty acres were more than I had hoped and prayed for. The owner's offer to reduce the $30,000 purchase price to $28,500 if I could raise the cash instead of his holding the mortgage, was deeply appreciated. Immediately we began to pray that God would provide loans from dedicated Christians that would cover the entire $28,500 and effect a $1,500 saving, by the deadline that had been set.

Those days at the chalet were beautiful in every way, but especially in the joy of a two-way devotional experience. God spoke day after day where the bookmark was, and it became increasingly exciting. Devotional dialog is *so* much more meaningful than the usual one-way experience!

I sat each morning beside that rushing trout stream and enjoyed my devotions more than I have ever enjoyed them at any other point in my life. God was there by that rushing stream too, speaking in a "still, small voice." Sometimes He spoke so clearly that I almost thought the words "still" and "small" inappropriate! His voice was *loud* and *clear*!

Early one morning, sitting in my favorite spot on the little bridge that crosses the stream as part of the entrance road, before opening my Bible where the bookmark was, I took everything in around me. I noted the refreshingly cool air almost pushing up against my chest. I recall thinking, "That air rising off the stream is cool like that because the stream comes from many mountain springs pouring their water into the ravine. It's cold, cold water!" I noted with great enjoyment the singing of a bird near its nest in one of the trees that hung so low over the water. That delightful little songbird changed his tune so frequently that I wondered whether or not there were mockingbirds in that part of the country.

I looked up toward the clear blue of the sky and observed that the sun was floodlighting the tips of the trees, high on the west side of the ravine. That sunshine would reach where I was sitting by the stream in about another half hour and would warm me. The first man-made sound interrupted the natural sounds of cascading water, singing bird, and soft breeze. It was the sound of a car. Further up the ravine, Clyde's son Bill, a flight instructor over at Moody Aviation, was backing his car around, preparing to leave for work. The car made its way up his driveway and then entered Tiger Creek Road. Bill drove down through the ravine, past where I was sitting, as he did each morning on his way to work. He waved as he passed.

After all of this I opened my Bible to the bookmarked page...

The waters...flowed over the mountains, they went down into the valleys, to the place you assigned for them...He makes springs pour water into the ravines: it flows between the mountains....The birds of the air nest by the waters; they sing among the branches...The sun rises, and...Then man goes out to his work. [71]

The goosebumps which rose on my flesh were *not* caused by the cool air arising from the mountain stream! God had spoken so forcefully and clearly as to thrill my soul deeply.

Does God really speak as clearly as that? How

direct is this line to and from heaven? Is dialog meant to be an occasional crisis intervention kind of thing, or does God enjoy speaking to us on a regular basis?

These are far from mystical questions. They bear upon the nitty-gritty of life. Perhaps they are the key to the abundant life, rather than great emotion-packed, exotic spiritual experiences. Perhaps God is still a God who speaks through the still, small voice of His Word, rather than through earthquake, wind and fire! This much I know, I felt His presence there. I felt it *there*, beside the churning stream, among the sun-dappled trees, in earshot of the song-filled bird He had created. A song welled up in my own soul, and that bird and I had a God-inspired duet.

Before leaving the chalet in Tennessee to return to Vancouver, there was another remarkable confirmation of the Lord's unseen hand in all of these events. One day Clyde suddenly asked me, "How did you happen to name it 'Fairhaven'? It isn't even spelled the Bible way, you know."

Yes, I did know that. In the Bible it was Fair Havens into which the ship sailed. No, I could not tell him how I had happened to name it Fairhaven, except that it described what I wanted the new ministry to be—a fair haven for those who needed it.

"Perhaps I can tell you," he said. "When the Lord prompted us to leave Ohio and move up into these mountains to build this chalet, we left the fellowship of the Fairhaven Alliance Church of

Dayton, Ohio. Little did we know that we were leaving Fairhaven to build Fairhaven!''

The four of us thrilled once again to realize that God's hand was in all of this in such minute detail. It added to our deepseated impressions that the entire project was a God-planned one, and we were happy participants in that exciting plan.

We resigned from the Vancouver church. We put our house up for sale. We advertised our furniture; there was no one to move us those three thousand miles. Fairhaven Ministries was a dream, not a reality as yet. It had no treasury! Who would pay the moving bill for a five-bedroom home? The best thing to do was to sell our 25-year accumulation of earthly things. They were, after all, just "things."

It's a little more easily said than done, but we found an amazing supply of grace for the task. I thought there would be tears when the organ was carried out of the house, for Elaine plays so beautifully and enjoyed sitting there, relaxing at the keyboard. There were no tears, though I cannot say how deep the inner feelings may have run as the men lugged the Hammond A-100 out the door.

In the middle of the disposition of our possessions, God spoke so sweetly one morning in devotions. I had prayed before opening my Bible where the bookmark was, "Lord Jesus, Elaine and I are asking You for a little home near Elizabethton, Tennessee, with some wooded area, close enough to Moody Aviation to be able to entertain the students. We are living in a very beautiful home on a perfect street. We are selling everything and leaving it behind. Somehow I believe in my heart that while earthly possessions are to have no hold on us, and we are easily to let them go for Your sake, You will not let a man and woman do that without turning around and providing so graciously for them. You said, 'You do not have because you do not ask God.'[72] I am asking very specifically for a little place, well kept, and within our price range. I remember that you said, 'No man gives up houses or lands, etc....' ''

My bookmark rested that morning at Matthew 19. Before the end of that very chapter I came to the words,

Everyone who has left houses or brothers or sisters or father or mother or children or fields for my sake will receive a hundred times as much and will inherit eternal life. [73]

My thrilled response was, "I am deeply humbled by the sweet ways in which You speak so clearly and so promptly. I love you *very* much."

With all this reassurance, a person should march forward easily to the thrill of God-given orders. I wish it were that easy for me! The house was sold, the furniture was selling fast, and my resignation from the church was public knowledge now. On October 1 my salary would cease. No support had been pledged, and I would *not* ask anyone for money. God would have to bring it in by prompting people.

When God had called our friends Billy and

Irene Ogg into His service with the Gospel Missionary Union, it was their responsibility to raise their own finances. They knew that the one thing they could not do was ask people for support. They did know how to ask God for it, however. They prayed and watched as God provided every cent that was needed.

Our support would have to come on that same basis. Surely God had sensitive Christians to whom He could speak who had the means to help. "Lord, we are not trying to be stubborn, or proud. We are simply asking You to do it by divine inspiration, rather than our doing it by human effort."

That all sounds beautiful and noble and spiritual, but the truth of the matter is that one morning I felt panic clutching at my throat! I cried out, "Lord, I'm scared! I don't know where our support is coming from. I don't know how we are going to be able to afford to put roads on the mountain, so we can begin to develop it (roads cost a lot of money!). I don't even have any guarantee that Christian workers will come to us after we get there. They are frequently workaholics. You can hardly get them to take a day off once a week, let alone taking off a week or two! Lord, I need reassurance. I know You have given it before, but You didn't get angry with Gideon when he asked You for further confirmation, and I dare come to You again for reassurance. So graciously You have spoken in my devotions before—do it again. Be patient with Your fearful servant!"

The bookmarked pages were far from a

disappointment!

Do not be afraid,...my servant,...Do not tremble, do not be afraid. Did I not proclaim this?....I will turn all my mountains into roads....See, they will come from afar—some from the north, some from the west....burst into song, O mountains! For the Lord comforts his people and will have compassion on his afflicted ones. [74]

All three of my stated concerns had been so specifically answered. I was so excited that I failed to catch the significance of the two missing directions. In the middle of the night I awakened, and mulling over how beautifully God had spoken, I was suddenly struck with the thought, "There were only two directions mentioned in those verses—what were they?"

I got out of bed, looked the passage up again and noted that the north and the west were mentioned and the south and the east had been omitted. Suddenly I realized that Fairhaven was to be in the southeastern portion of the U.S. and probably most of our guests would come from the north and the west. (As of this writing, we have had in excess of 200 guests and all but 18 of them have come from the north and the west, just as God predicted!)

It is embarrassing to tell you the truth here. With all of this behind us, we *still* had our moments of doubt. It is difficult not to have spasms of fear when you are facing something altogether new and totally uncharted. Who had ever done this before? Where could we get advice? When and from whence would our support be forthcoming? How long must we move forward by faith alone, with nothing tangible to go on? *Lord, help me!*

When God has spoken and you *know* He has....

When directions are clear, and you *know* they are....

But in contrast...

When hoped for sources did not materialize and you *know* they didn't...

When the finances are not there, and you *know* they aren't...

WHAT THEN?

How can you maintain faith purely on the basis of the One you trust, while the days slip away relentlessly and the deadlines draw nearer? *"Why should we doubt, He has never failed us yet!"* But with six weeks remaining until we were to drive away from that house, we had not one cent of promised support. *"Surely God has a home all prepared for us down there in Tennessee!"* But item by item our home in Vancouver was disintegrating and the accumulation of 25 years was crumbling. *"God has reassured us three times now from His Word!"* But the hours changed into days, and the days into weeks, and there had not been received one promised loan to help pay on the property, and there was not one cent of promised support.

I did not feel I could ask for a reassurance again. Even Gideon had been content with two confirmations of the Lord's will for him, and we had already had three (or more). I reminded my heart of those confirmations: "You still the hunger of those you cherish...." "Do not be afraid, my servant. Did I not proclaim (order) this?" "Everyone who has left...for my sake will receive...."

My heart said, "Lord, I've never felt more like a twin brother to the man in Mark 9:24 than right now, 'Lord I believe, help my unbelief!' " God heard that prayer, and began that very day to reassure in tangible ways. I will list them:

August 20 (that very day): A letter from someone in Washington State pledging $50 a month.

August 26: A card from a couple out of work at the moment, saying they would be trusting God for $25 a month for our support.

August 28: A letter from an elderly widow in California confirming her desire to give a sacrificial $6 per month.

August 29: A promise from a professional couple in Vancouver to back us with $100 a month.

August 29: A phone call from the chairman of the missionary committee at the Meadow Creek Baptist Church in Anoka, Minnesota, confirming a $500 per month commitment!

By the end of August 1979, $681 per month had been pledged. God is never late, though our faith is sometimes tested. In addition to this the following encouragements came:

August 29: A phone call from a preacher in a

small church. He said he would like to loan Fairhaven $1,000 to help pay for that land.

August 29 (later that same day): A phone call from a doctor. He would like to loan us $8,000 for the same purpose.

August ? (the date is not recorded in my diary): A $50 gift from a secretary to help pay for the land—$1 for each acre as an encouragement to believe for what God would do in future days!

"Dear Lord, You are so faithful...and so patient with my inability to trust when I do not see," I prayed. "Thank you for being what You are! How true is Your Word, 'If we are faithless, He will remain faithful!' " [75]

It was at this point that we asked the Lord to give to us principles upon which Fairhaven Ministries could be established and could operate so as to bring maximum glory to His own name. Since He was so undeniably the Founder of the organization, we wanted those principles to come from Him. The following was drawn up and printed for distribution to interested friends:

1. Fairhaven Ministries will be conducted as directed by God's very personal supervision. His Word and the advice of godly people will be considered carefully.

2. The mailing list will be composed of persons who have specifically asked to be placed there, or who have demonstrated a more than ordinary interest in this ministry. No one will be bothered with

mail he does not want.

3. Funds will be prayed in. No appeals for funds are to be characterized by pressure. Fairhaven will be a faith ministry in the fullest sense of the Word.

4. New ministries will be added only as indicated by the Lord, and confirmed by a provision of staff or of special enablings. No additional staff will be sought. God must confirm their addition.

5. Indebtedness shall be avoided except as equity clearly and generously covers the indebtedness.

Only one of the above listed principles seemed to be possibly a little too idealistic. Would we someday regret having put into print the idea that we would not be seeking additional staff members? The day might come when we would need someone and would want to make a search for the right person. But then, the Lord could bring to us the needed personnel just as He had brought Clyde and Marguerite and Elaine and I together, couldn't He? We included the principle.

A year later, we were so sure of the leading of the Lord in including that, for we had had nearly 60 persons who had inquired seriously about joining our staff someday. These include licensed psychologists, maintenance people, business administrators, secretaries, and others.

Regarding the principle that speaks of praying in the funds, I realize that I was influenced by reading about that saint of the last century,

George Muller. He would not appeal to man for funds, but made his requests to God alone. So marvelously God answered prayer that every need was met, and more importantly, God was wonderfully glorified in it all. What I did not realize at the time of listing those principles, was that Mr. Muller had been influenced by another person (Mr. A.H. Franke) who 100 years earlier had established an orphanage on those very same principles.[76] If Mr. Muller's life had been so strongly influenced by a man who lived 100 years earlier, why should not we in this century permit a strong influence upon our lives by Muller's nineteenth century example?

I was rehearsing some of these exciting events to a friend one day, when he said, "That sounds like L'Abri." I hated to admit that I had never read *L'Abri*, for most of the church people had!

Immediately I checked the book out of the church library. The account intrigued me, especially as I saw the similarities in the Lord's leadings. I was especially encouraged to note that He had directed us to adopt a set of principles almost identical to the ones adopted at L'Abri. It made me all the more certain that they were from God, and not our own thinking.

I wish to leave the fantastic sequel to this divinely inspired beginning for another book. To close this section, I want to share one more word from heaven that came in such a special way. It seemed almost a capstone to all the other times God had spoken.

I felt overwhelmed one morning with the

definiteness of God's words to my heart. Before opening my Bible where the bookmark was, I prayed, and I wrote my prayer out in full, "Lord, I ask You questions and You answer them. I tell You my fears and You relieve them. I ask for reassurances and You give them. Today I tell You nothing. I ask for nothing. I just listen for Your instructions, or rebuke, or expression of love. It will need to have its own appropriateness without my initiation of thoughts...I'm listening, Lord."

I opened to read, and to my amazement found these words in my devotional reading for that morning:

I revealed myself to those who did not ask for me; I was found by those who did not seek me...To (those who)...did not call on my name, I said, "Here am I, here am I." [77]

How special! *God Himself*, not directions, or promises, or confirmations, but *far more* than all of that—God Himself! Shouldn't that be the ultimate goal in our search for His will? We should not be looking so much for directions for living, or promises of blessing, or confirmations of specific decisions without our overriding goal being that of coming ever closer to the One Who in love is calling out to us, "Here I am! Here I am!"

As I look back over the details of the Fairhaven story, I am struck by the fact that all nine of the "ways the Lord leads" listed in Section II were used of God to bring about this special work of God. God inspired Fairhaven the dream first, and then through special directions effected a transformation of a dream into Fairhaven the incorporated, I.R.S.-approved reality with a staff and a Board of Directors, and a chalet to use.

Remember with me the ways by which God had led:

1. Roadblocks (or closed doors): Remember the sale of the eleven acres in Vancouver that slowed the progress there.

2. Remarkable revelations: Remember how He revealed His own planning by having the chalet already built and ready to go according to His own timetable instead of ours, and revealed it so dramatically.

3. Difficult experiences: Remember the letters I received from new workers who were encountering snags that threatened to take them out of the ministry. These inspired the dream.

4. Specific instructions: Remember the challenge God gave to obey Him by following a drastic change of orders ("You are not the one.")

5. Sanctified reason: Remember the trip to Tennessee to meet the Powells to see if our personalities were compatible.

6. The counsel of godly people: Remember the letters to fourteen district superintendents and the consultation with Dr. Bailey.

7. Devotional application: Remember the many times Scripture passages were used so pointedly by God to give both leading and confirmation of those leadings.

8. Open doors (or answers to prayers): Remember the phone call from Clyde Powell after seven days of specific prayer.

97

9. Inner peace: Remember the numerous times when inner turmoil was the natural by-product of what was happening, and then the Lord through His reassurances restored an inner peace. In the account I have not emphasized as I might have the supernatural peace He gave, except in the incident of the selling of the organ.

The Fairhaven account is far from finished at this point, for God provided in the most amazing manner through sensitive people during the first year of operation. Fairhaven is being greatly used of the Lord in the lives of Christian workers and laymen. The portion of the account reported here is sufficient for the purposes of this book, and I will leave the full story for another time.

I have in this section attempted to let God's workings illustrate the truth that *He loves to reveal His will to His children*. Can we honestly conclude otherwise in the face of the overwhelming evidence?

Section IV

GOD'S WILL
How Can I Find It?

Are there specific steps I can take to find God's will for my life?

I believe there are. This section essentially comprises a checklist for you to consider. Perhaps it will point out some missing ingredient in your quest for a knowledge of the will of God for you. As you consider each of the suggestions, ask yourself, "How do I measure up in reference to this specific bit of advice?"

1. *Clarify your concept of God.* "I love you, I *love* you, I LOVE YOU!" is the message God persistently asserts throughout the Scriptures. Out of His great heart of love there flows a desire to communicate with you. He *wants* you to know His will, and delights to reveal it to you. Be thoroughly convinced of that. I agree 100 percent with Margaret Erb who insists, "Every time you are faced with making an important decision you can know His will."[78]

2. *Memorize Scripture that reflects His nature.* This will help you to fix firmly in your mind a

clear, accurate, beautiful concept of the God you serve. "I have loved you with an everlasting love" (Jeremiah 31:3). "God demonstrates His own love for us in this: while we were still sinners, Christ died for us" (Romans 5:8). "Peace I leave with you, my peace I give you. I do not give to you as the world gives" (John 14:27). "As the Father has loved me, so have I loved you" (John 15:9).

3. *Memorize Scripture that promises you a revelation of His will.* "I will instruct you and teach you in the way you should go; I will counsel you and watch over you" (Psalm 32:8). "You will be able to test and approve what God's will is—his good, pleasing, and perfect will" (Romans 12:2b). "You will guide me with your counsel" (Psalm 73:24a). "Trust in the Lord with all your heart and lean not on your own understanding; in all your ways acknowledge him, and he will make your paths straight" (or "will direct your paths" KJV) (Proverbs 3:5,6).

4. *Follow His revealed will now.* Today! Remember that a very high percentage of the will of God for your life is clearly revealed in His Word. By faithfully following that *revealed* will, you will gain a growing confidence that His *concealed* will, will surely be made plain. Consciously work at obeying the promptings of God's Spirit in every little detail. God loves to reveal more of His will to obedient sons and daughters!

Robert Oertler Jr., in his essay "Undebatable

Guidance," suggests, "If we learn to obey God where His will is obvious, we'll develop the ability to sense His will where the specific word is not so obvious. The more we live in joyful obedience to the Lord, the more we'll discern His likes and dislikes."[79]

Carl Thomas says, "Lives lived every moment for Christ are so occupied with proving or experiencing the outworking of God's will now that there is not time to be vexed about what God is going to do next year or next week."[80]

Oliver Barclay is emphatic in stating, "Only committed Christians are promised any guidance at all."[81] To put it bluntly—if you are unwilling to obey what God has already revealed to you, you should not expect to learn anything new from God about what is best and right for your future!

5. *Refuse to fear the revelation of God's will.* There are certain concepts which need to be evaluated carefully by any discerning Christian. The first could be stated as, *"God will ask me to do something I don't want to do."* Perhaps He will, but not without enabling, and certainly not without exciting results for you. *"God may not want me to do the thing I so deeply want to do."* Perhaps you are right, but God's direction is in your best interests. It is not a turn of events to fear. Rather than falling into this kind of thinking, remind yourself continually that there is nothing to fear in God's will for you.

There is no *safer place* for you than in God's will. There is no *better place* for you than in God's will. There is no more *productive place* for you than in God's will. You need to share Paul Fromer's conviction that, "The safest and most satisfying place in the world is dead center in the will of Christ."[82]

6. *Be certain you sincerely want His will.* This is a step beyond refusing to fear the revelation of His will. It is essential. Do not expect God to reveal His will to you so you can make a decision about it as to what you will do (follow it, or reject it). "My food is to do the will of him who sent me," the Lord Jesus said! "Lord, I want what You want," must be sincerely expressed.

You must have a genuine commitment to wanting His will, not half-heartedly, but with all your heart. A little girl acknowledged a gift from her aunt with these words, "Thank you for your present. I have always wanted a pin cushion, but not very much."[83] The heart that desires the will of God with reservations ought to be honest enough to admit its affinity with that little girl!

Robert Oertler Jr. makes the point very tersely when he writes, "It's useless to search for God's will if you're unwilling to obey. Often we waste our time in an agony of searching. We kid ourselves. But we don't kid God who knows that we really don't intend to obey."[84]

The Bible says, "If anyone chooses to do God's will...."[85] Notice that it is not, "If anyone chooses to *find* God's will." The choice must be to *do*, rather than to *find*! Remember that God "guides guidable people, just the same as he teaches teachable people."[86]

7. *Read your Bible consistently.* Make daily Bible reading as much a part of your daily life as your meals. The Israelites needed to gather manna daily—so do you! God can speak to you through your daily reading in exciting ways, as He has to others. He is no respecter of persons.

Dr. Bright, in the article quoted earlier, places a heavy stress upon this method of determining God's will. He writes, "I cannot stress enough the importance of getting to know and responding to the perfect, holy, sovereign mind of God through regular, Spirit-led study and application of His Word."[87]

In connection with letting God speak to you through His Word, you may frequently hear the warning sounded, "Be very careful of lifting a verse out of its context." Most of us have listened to people who were obviously clutching some portion of a verse and calling it God's direction. Even as we are listening to that person rehearse with emotion that portion of the text to us, we cannot quite believe that we would interpret it in the same way. We smile politely, and turn a bit further away from this method of determining God's will for our own lives.

I agree with the caution that is offered, but I feel there is another side to that coin of truth. Examine it with me. When I am listening for God's voice to my heart, I do not burden myself down with hermeneutical earmuffs. I don't keep asking myself, "What was the meaning of the text as originally given?" or "To whom did God first speak these words?" or "What about the context in which I find this text?" Frankly, I could

105

hardly care less about the answers to these questions initially.

When I have thoroughly enjoyed the thrill of hearing God's voice, so pertinent to the situation, and have responded to Him in prayer, then I look to see if there are yet additional lessons for me in the context or in the historical setting, or whatever. Finding none, I do not discard the word from heaven as irrelevant.

While registrar at the St. Paul Bible College, Dr. Donald Bierle, a man with a keen mind and impressive training, gave his testimony to a group of pastors in Indiana where we were both speaking. I empathized with the man as he described his intellectual struggles. The climax of it all came one night while he was reading from the book of Job. "Suddenly God was no longer talking to Job—He was talking to me!" Dr. Bierle said. "I found myself on my knees crying, with a deeply emotional thought possessing me, 'Lord, I'm sorry!' Almost immediately there followed another profoundly emotional response, 'Thank You, Lord—thank You!'"

"Suddenly God was no longer talking to Job, He was talking to me!" I feel those words are deeply significant. Let God talk to *you* through His Word. There are moments so rare and valuable and delicious and memorable as to enrich life immeasurably that are missed by many a hesitant Christian. You do not have to fear this method of discerning God's plan for you. There are checks and controls you can use to be certain it is the voice of God and not simply your responsiveness to words that tend to reinforce some personal desire of yours. We will mention these later in this section.

I stay with this suggestion longer than most, because I feel it is very important. Margaret Erb makes a point we ought not to miss in her essay "God Has a Plan" when she says that God "has access to your thought life in a way that no other person has. He can influence your actions by guiding your thoughts. As you read His Word and fellowship with Him in prayer, He is given access to your thoughts to a degree which is impossible when you are tearing around with your daily duties."[88]

The person who is serious about discovering God's will for his life should be as consistent in his Bible reading as the pianist who is serious about making a career of his music is in his daily practice. If you are not, you need to question the depth of your desire to know God's will for you.

8. *Ask God to fill you with His Holy Spirit.* Wisdom, guidance, and discernment are all ministries of the Holy Spirit of God to the believer. "When he, the Spirit of truth, comes, he will guide you into all truth....He will tell you what is yet to come" (John 16:13).

In some ways it makes more sense to ask God for discernment than it does to ask for direction in a specific instance. The former will serve you well in each instance of decision-making you face. The latter is only for one particular instance.

The suggestion to ask God to fill you with His Holy Spirit may raise a lot of questions in your mind. You may have been struggling with this biblical concept for a long time. We have a tendency to make some of the most helpful truths of God's Word far more complex than He ever intended. Our salvation is so simple that people have stumbled over it since the early Greeks who thought the preaching of the cross "foolishness" because it was not complex enough to suit their minds. They loved intricate reasoning!

The truth of being filled with the Holy Spirit is so simple that well meaning Christians wrestle and struggle with truth they should be enjoying.

God has said plainly, "If you then, though you are evil, know how to give good gifts to your children, how much more will your Father in heaven give the Holy Spirit to those who ask him!"[89] With regard to their salvation, most Christians claimed a promise like John 1:12: "Yet to all who received him, to those who believed in his name, he gave the right to become children of God." I suggest you take a simple promise like the one given at the beginning of this paragraph and claim it for the experience of being filled with His Holy Spirit. Claim that promise by simple faith, as you claimed another for your salvation.

No one can be more certain of God's will than the person who is filled with the "Spirit of Truth" who will "guide you into all truth."

9. *Specifically ask Him to reveal His will to you.* "You do not have because you do not ask God," James states bluntly.[90] In just as forthright a manner, he insists, "If you want to know what God wants you to do, ask him, and he will gladly tell you, for he is always ready to give a bountiful

supply of wisdom to all who ask him; he will not resent it."[91]

10. *Exercise your faith.* That same passage in the first chapter of James goes right on to say, "But when you ask him, be sure that you really expect him to tell you, for a doubtful mind will be as unsettled as a wave of the sea that is driven and tossed by the wind; and every decision you then make will be uncertain, as you turn first this way, and then that. If you don't ask with faith, don't expect the Lord to give you any solid answer."[92]

Discipline your heart and mind to have an expectant attitude. You have a solid basis for doing this. God's Word is reassuring—strongly reassuring! "This God is our God for ever and ever; *he will be our guide* even to the end" (italics added).[93] God responds to faith. It pleases Him. Without it, it is impossible to please Him.[94] Exercise your faith!

11. *Weigh the circumstances.* Opened or closed doors *can* be very significant as a part of the method God uses to direct your life. Margaret Erb brings the role of circumstances into focus when she writes, "If we are always to be guided by circumstances alone we would make many wrong decisions. But where situations in which we find ourselves, or influences which come into our lives confirm the decisions which we are coming to through prayer and Bible study, we may take them as an added evidence of God's guidance."[95]

I like Oswald Chambers's reminder that God is "the Master Engineer of circumstances."[96] I have discovered with excitement that most of the doors that swing closed or open in my pathway swing on divine hinges. This serendipity has made life a grand adventure for me.

12. *Do not expect God to speak dramatically*, (though he may!). Speaking dramatically to His children is the unusual, not the norm. God seldom speaks in a loud voice. His manner is generally soft-spoken. Even Elijah had to learn that God is not always the God of the wind, the earthquake, and the fire! When God dealt with Elijah in a very personal way about his relationship to Himself, He allowed a "great and powerful wind (to tear) the mountains apart and shatter the rocks...but *the Lord was not in the wind.*" Then God sent an earthquake, "but *the Lord was not in the earthquake.*" "After the earthquake came a fire, but *the Lord was not in the fire.* And after the fire came *a gentle whisper*"[97] (italics added in each instance).

Elijah had prayed through for rain to return to the land, and had seen it accompanied by *wind.*[98] He had had the *earthshaking* experience of raising a dead boy into life again.[99] He had prayed down the *fire* upon the sacrifice there on Mount Carmel in the sight of the prophets of Baal.[100] Now God was saying to him, "Elijah, I am not always found in the wind, the earthquake, and the fire. But I *am* always there, if you will listen for my whisper!" Comparatively few Christians have tuned their spiritual ears to hear the whisper of God. Those who have are greatly enriched.

110

On occasion God has led me in dramatic ways, but those times have been rare delights and not daily or even regular occurrences. "Most of us at some time or other have longed for...the overwhelming bolt from the blue. But God normally doesn't reveal His will in these ways," Robert Oertler Jr. insists. [101]

13. *Obey step by step what He reveals.* Why should God reveal anything further to you if there is something He has already revealed that you are not obeying? I am convinced that the words "every little detail" are tremendously significant. Obedience in a small step will prepare the way for easier obedience to the big steps He indicates you should take.

14. *Test your proposed decision by submitting it to godly Christian friends who know you well*, if you wish. You may want confirmation from spiritually qualified persons, but you should not develop such a dependency relationship with other mature Christians that you cannot make a decision without them. Use them wisely and sparingly.

I seldom finalize a major decision without consulting with friends whom I consider to be spiritually mature and sensitive. I do not ask them to take the responsibility for my decision in any way—that's *my* responsibility. I simply use them as a sounding board, and for their godly counsel.

In the last 23 years of his life (beginning at age 70), George Muller left his orphanage work in the hands of others and traveled the world over, preaching to huge crowds. He did this at what he felt was the Lord's direction. There were those who questioned this and asked why he did not stay at home to supervise the work of the Ashley Down Houses. He answered, "Very godly and advanced Christians have told me that they consider my present labors the most important of my whole life." [102] This became confirmation enough for that godly man.

15. *Don't let reverses shake your confidence.* Once God has revealed His will to you and you feel confident of that, pursue it with diligence and don't be swayed by the difficulties you encounter. The disciples were in the will of God, and yet they found themselves in the middle of a terrible storm. "Teacher, don't you care if we drown?" they cried. [103] They had cast away their confidence, even though the Lord Himself was in the boat with them! Is it any wonder that we should from time to time unwisely cast away ours?!

By contrast, in the will of God Paul found himself in a horrible storm with "winds of hurricane force." Even the seasoned sailors had given up all hope of being saved. An angel from God reassured Paul, and in the middle of that hurricane Paul was able to shout above the sound of the howling winds and the creaking boards and the crashing, smashing waves, "Keep up your courage men, for I have faith in God that it will happen just as he told me." [104]

God had reassured him that he would stand trial before Caesar in Rome, and he knew that there wasn't a storm on earth that could keep him from getting there! His confidence would not be shaken by circumstances. It was based on something more solid than circumstances—a word from God!

My greatest hero of faith and trust and implicit obedience to the will of God is George Muller. Three years before his death at 93, looking back over his life he wrote, "I never remember, in all my Christian course, a period now...of sixty-nine years and four months, that I ever SINCERELY AND PATIENTLY sought to know the will of God by *the teaching of the Holy Ghost*, through *the instrumentality of the Word of God*, but I have been ALWAYS directed rightly. But if *honesty of heart* and *uprightness before God* were lacking, or if I did not *patiently* wait upon God for instruction, or if I preferred *the counsel of my fellow men* to the declarations of *the Word of the living God*, I made great mistakes" [105] (italics his).

I look back over my half-as-long life and rejoice to be able to say that it is as true in the twentieth century as it was in the nineteenth! George Muller's God is *my* God, *and yours*. He is just as eager to reveal His will to us as He was to him, when we are careful to know, understand and follow the conditions and processes.

May God encourage you as you seek His will for your life. Remember this: The happiest, most fruitful, most meaningful life is the one that is lived according to the plan God mapped out long ages ago. It is spent primarily for God, and secondarily for others, and lastly for yourself.

*J*esus, and *O*thers, and *Y*ou—what a wonderful
way to spell JOY!

Section V

GOD'S WILL
How Contemporary is It?

God leads His committed children. In fact, He *loves* to, no doubt about it! Some of the methods He uses were listed for you in Section II. Illustrations were given in that section that adequately illuminated the points.

In this section I go back over that list to illustrate again that God is *currently* active in these ways. He is guiding Christian people in ways that prove His love and thrill their hearts—and will thrill yours.

The vignettes presented in this final section are arranged to correspond with the order of the list previously presented. My intention is to strengthen your confidence in the personal interest of God in your life.

GOD LEADS BY CLOSED DOORS

A series of meetings in Hamlet, Nebraska, was to be followed by a men's retreat at Glen Eyrie (the Navigator's fabulous castle in Colorado

Springs). Two days and one night would be mine to do with as I pleased between those two speaking engagements.

A delightful idea came to mind. I would rent a car and head for Estes Park, Colorado. I would find a cabin with a fireplace and would hibernate for 24 hours, preparing myself spiritually before heading on to Glen Eyrie and my commitment there. Pastor and Mrs. Dennis Gordon of the Hamlet Union Church insisted that I use their car instead of renting one. He would get it back at the men's retreat. How nice of them! For weeks beforehand I relished the thought of that time alone in the mountains beside a cozy fire.

The meetings were completed in Hamlet on Wednesday night. Thursday morning I was ready to set out for Estes Park, but the weatherman said that a storm was moving into northern Colorado. I quickly changed my plans. I would go south, toward Colorado Springs instead of Estes Park, hopeful of avoiding the storm.

Arriving in Colorado Springs, I checked with the chamber of commerce as to where there might be a cottage with a fireplace. They named two places for me. Checking them out, I discovered that one was closed for the season, and the other looked rather shabby. I drove on up the mountains to Woodland Park and tried to find something there. My precious hours were slipping away as I searched, and I was coming up with nothing suitable. "Lord Jesus, You know how much I would like to have a place with a fireplace. I don't understand why I am having such trouble. Please help me!" I prayed.

But nothing turned up. Snow began to swirl lazily in front of my headlights. I decided it would be better to go back down the mountain, and not chance getting stuck up on that mountain and missing my speaking engagement at Glen Eyrie.

I felt a keen disappointment as I drove the winding road down the mountain. I really tried to remember that God can be in our disappointments as well as in our joys, but it's not easy to be completely victorious in the midst of disappointment. The deeper the disappointment, the more God-given grace is needed to be thoroughly victorious!

Coming through Manitou Springs on my way up the mountain, I had noted the various motels. The nicest among them had been The Villa. I didn't consider stopping there, for I assumed it would be too expensive. I always try to use Fairhaven's funds carefully. As I passed by The Villa, I felt a sudden urge to turn in and check their prices. As I jerked the steering wheel to the right, I did not think of that urge as divine prompting. It was simply a recalling of the fact that sometimes (not often) the nicer places are not much more costly than the shabbier ones. At least there was no harm in checking!

A nice young fellow named Mark was at the desk. The price? $20 per night. "May I see a room?" I asked, trying not to show too much pleasure at the reasonable price! The room was really very nice. "I'll take it!" I said with the definiteness that comes from being decidedly pleased. "For one night?" Mark asked. "Yes," I said, "Tomorrow I am going over to Glen Eyrie to

119

speak to a group of men there.'' "What will you be speaking about?'' he asked. "Well,'' I said, "It's a group of church men, and I'll be speaking to them from the Bible.'' Mark's face lit up as he said, "I'm a Christian brethren, too!'' I wasn't certain whether that was a denomination or a person, but I suspected it was meant to be a person.

"Tell me about it, Mark. How did you become a Christian?'' I asked. His answer thrilled me. "It happened shortly after my brother was killed by a car. I was so deeply shocked and hurt. I felt desperately that I had to find meaning and truth somehow, so I began a diligent search. No matter how hard I tried, I could not seem to find truth or meaning, however.

"On my way to class one day at college, I said to myself, 'I cannot find meaning and truth by myself. I have exhausted all my resources. If they are to be found, somehow they are going to have to come to me!'

"When I arrived at class, a motivational tape was being played. The speaker was interesting and I enjoyed the things he had to say. At the very end of his talk, he made one statement that startled me. He suggested that we should read our Bibles every day! Immediately there was a response within me. Perhaps that's it! Perhaps the meaning of life and genuine truth is to be found in the Bible.

"There had been a Bible at the head of my bed for a long time, but I had not read it. I picked it up with intense excitement. I opened to the first page and read, 'Pope Leo XIII granted to the faithful who shall read for at least a quarter of an hour the books of the Sacred Scripture with the veneration due to the Divine Word, and as spiritual reading, an indulgence of 300 days.' '' [106]

He was quoting from memory. I startled him by joining right in with him, word for word! "Oh, are you a Catholic, too?" he asked. I could have answered, "No, but I am a Christian brethren." Actually, I said, "No, Mark, but our earthly affiliations are not what is important. It is our relationship to the living Christ that makes the difference." I could both see and sense his agreement with me.

"I didn't know the meaning of the word 'indulgence,' " he continued, "but it seemed like a warm word. I turned to the next page where I read something about the Holy Spirit providing illumination to the sincere reader, and suddenly I felt overwhelmed with it all.

"With great excitement I realized that I had found meaning. I had found the source of truth! The room glowed with a light, and filled with a wonderful Presence, and in that moment I was reborn. The Holy Spirit did indeed come to instruct me, and to interpret to me. He showed me that these two sections, the Old Testament and the New Testament, were first prophecy, and then prophecy fulfilled. He showed me the importance of studying the Scriptures."

I am slow to accept testimonies of great lights, and visionary experiences. But my heart was so thrilled with the vibrance and vitality of this new Christian's understanding of the truth, as he went on to share with me, sprinkling his comments liberally with familiar scriptures that had become a part of him through diligent study, that I felt a witness in my own spirit that this was very genuine.

"Mark, what time do you finish here at the desk?" I asked. "At ten o'clock," he said. "How about coming up to my room and we will have prayer there together," I suggested. He was pleased. We spent nearly an hour together in fellowship and prayer that night. It was a beautiful experience for us both.

What happened to *my* plans for a cottage with a fireplace? By direct intervention, God had replaced them with something that warmed my heart instead of my toes. I had been privileged to strengthen Mark Dolan's hand in the Lord. As two "Christian brethren" we had shared and prayed together. I went on my way to Glen Eyrie the next day rejoicing. By *closed doors* God had so beautifully directed my footsteps!

GOD LEADS BY
REMARKABLE REVELATIONS

Arnold Reimer felt almost overwhelmed with the enormity of the challenge that lay ahead of him. He was the pastor of the Avenue Road Church of The Christian and Missionary Alliance in Toronto, Canada. The church was located in an area of the city that had changed drastically from former years. There was no off-the-street parking for the parishioners. Attendance had dwindled, and the congregation of that once great church was now a greatly reduced group that seemed to rattle around in a large, old building. Without relocation the future was dismal. Architect's plans seemed sometimes like daydreams. It was difficult to muster faith to believe that such could become a reality.

At the General Council of the denomination in St. Paul, Minnesota, Pastor and Mrs. Reimer were sitting at a table in a restaurant with friends. He confided in them the great crushing burden he carried. He felt so overcome by it all that he could not keep the tears from flowing. His wife and their friends began to cry, too! He felt embarrassed for them all.

Another friend, totally unaware of the situation and how pressing their personal need was, suggested that the Reimers come up to his motel room that night for a time of fellowship and prayer with some other delegates. They gladly accepted the invitation.

During the fellowship time in that room, a stranger to the Reimers began to share something that amazed them. "During the communion service this morning, I had a vision," he began. "It was so clear and definite that I fully expected Dr. Bailey to stop the service and say, 'There is someone that has something to share with us.' But he didn't do that, so I kept it to myself and pondered the meaning. In my vision I saw a large stone church...." He went on to describe the church in detail and Pastor Reimer recognized the description as fitting the Avenue Road Church perfectly. He continued, "The church was resting on the palm of a man's hand. The man was straining with all his might to lift the church higher, but in spite of all his straining and struggling, he was unable to lift it up.

"Then in another scene I saw the man (in proper proportion to the church now), his hand still outstretched with palm up, walking through the door of that church. As he was about to enter, a dove flew down and rested on his hand. With that dove in his hand, he entered the church. Out through the open windows of the church I saw the wingtips of the dove extending, until the wings were outstretched from the windows and the body of the dove was inside. Then gently those wings began to flap, and ever so gently the dove effortlessly did what the man had been unable to do!"

The point was so obvious to Pastor Reimer. Even as he told me the story, my own heart was deeply moved by the principle so graphically and beautifully illustrated.

The man continued to speak, telling further of his vision. "Then I saw another scene. The stones of that great church were displaced in orderly fashion and moved to an entirely different location. It was a beautiful, country-like situation. As I watched, I saw those stones come together to form a low, modern building." The man described something very similar to the architect's rendering of the proposed new Bayview Glen Church. "I saw crowds of people going in and out of the building," he concluded.

Pastor Reimer told me that when he left the room that night, he had his reassurance from heaven that God would indeed effect the miracle needed for the Avenue Road Church to be transformed into the very beautiful Bayview Glen Church it is today.

God still leads by remarkable revelations, even those of us who are not "given to" visions and dreams and similar things. God's sovereignty to work as He wills, and His great variety of workings thrill and excite me.

GOD LEADS BY DIFFICULT EXPERIENCES

The evangelical church in a certain small Polish town doesn't resemble a typical American church. It has no stained-glass windows, no steeple, no pews. A passerby can barely distinguish the large, two-story, rectangular structure from the homes that surround it. But the simple building stands out as a testimony of God's miraculous work in Poland today. It's a house that God built.

When the congregation of about forty people applied to build a church, authorities refused the needed approval. They applied time after time, but each time were told, "You cannot build a church." The believers would not give up; instead, they took a great step in boldness. "Since we can't build a church, we'll build a house," said Jan, the young pastor.

The group then submitted blueprints for a house to the authorities and began plans for construction. The authorities, however, imposed rigid building standards. They specified that the cement for the foundation had to be twice as strong as that of any normal house. In addition, the steel beams for the structure had to be twice as strong as those required for a home.

The congregation discovered that these materials could not be found anywhere in the country. All the cement in Poland had vanished; steel had also disappeared. The reason? The Soviet Union had purchased all available cement and steel for construction of the Olympic site in Moscow.

The believers still did not give in. They managed to find six bags of cement. In faith, they decided to start pouring the foundation, remembering the miracle of the loaves and fishes.

The day they began mixing the cement for the foundation, a woman from the neighborhood dropped by. Jan, a stocky, brown-haired man in his early thirties, was mixing the cement. The woman told him she had some cement stored in her garage, and volunteered to sell him nine bags. Jan was elated. After further conversation, the woman discovered that the group was building a church. "I can't sell you nine bags of cement," the woman said, "but I can *give you eighteen bags* of cement!"

That afternoon, Pastor Jan heard through a friend that another man in town had some cement. He approached the man, who donated an additional eight bags. The congregation now had enough cement to pour the entire foundation.

The building also required steel girders to support the second floor. The inspectors demanded that the "I" beams be thicker and heavier than what was normally needed. Such material was not available anywhere. Again the believers refused to concede. Instead, they prayed.

A friend came to Pastor Jan soon afterwards. He said he knew a steel worker who could acquire the steel girders. However, upon checking, they found that the girders were two centimeters wider and also heavier than required by the rigid building standards. But these were all that were available, and the believers accepted them gratefully.

Construction soon got under way. All able members of the small congregation shared in the labor. Their problems were far from over, however. Building inspectors constantly harassed the project. Each time an inspector discovered any defect or deviation from the submitted blueprint, he demanded that the workers tear down that part of the structure and start over again. But the believers persevered for two years, toiling and praying, until the building was completed in the spring of 1978.

After the building was completed, the congregation received word from the authorities that they could now build their church. Joyfully, they submitted their new prayer house for registration as a church, only to be told that since the building was constructed as a house, it would first have to meet the stringent structural standards for a church or public building.

The "house" was minutely inspected, and the officials were amazed to find that the foundation with the double-strength cement met their standards perfectly, as did all other features. But imagine the elation of the congregation when they discovered that the extra two centimeters on the steel girders gave them precisely the minimum size permitted for such a structure!

The "unreasonable" demands and harassment of the officials produced the kind of building the inspectors had to accept! Today, a happy Polish congregation is meeting in *the house that God planned and built.* [107]

Through difficult experiences, God so directly led those people!

GOD LEADS BY SPECIFIC INSTRUCTIONS

Listening to God's revealed principles, standards, and instructions is tremendously important. There is no surer and safer way to determine God's will for you than to get to know Him as personally and deeply as you can through acquaintance with His Word.

As a sincere young Christian, I heard a preacher say from the pulpit on the questionable basis of Philippians 4:19, "Remember, the promise is to provide for all your *needs*—it doesn't say for all your *wants!*" I went home and dutifully examined my prayer list and evaluated each item on it. Some were obviously wants, like the album of Fred Waring's Pennsylvanians singing beautiful hymn arrangements. I crossed these kinds of items off the list. I had not yet

128

learned to evaluate for myself each "truth" presented to me from the pulpit, to see how it measured up with biblical concepts in general, and not just with the one proof text offered.

Through specific instructions recorded in His Word, God began to correct this faulty teaching. I read, "You do not have, because you do not ask." [108] That began to trouble me. Did that verse apply only to my *needs*, and not to my *wants*? Then I came across a scripture that read, "They that seek the Lord shall not want any good thing." [109] I particularly noted that word "want." The more I became acquainted with His Word, the more I realized that God was a loving and gracious God. He was as gracious as any living man, and more so.

When my boys were small, they were always excited when I came home from a trip. I wasn't so naive as to think that all that excitement was because they were so happy to see me, though we were always happy to see one another again! They had come to expect a gift, on the basis of my past performance. That gift had better not be a new pair of shoes! I provided for their *wants*, and not just for their *needs*. Was I more gracious than God? Never! I realized that I had been very wrong to cross my wants off that prayer list. I knew that my Heavenly Father loved to provide for both needs and wants.

Just prior to revising my prayer list again to include some of those wants, God did an especially sweet thing. It was as though He were trying to make it extra clear to me that He was more loving and gracious than that preacher had

129

made Him out to be!

I had been ill with pneumonia, and had been absent from my desk at the American Cyanamid Company for a couple of weeks. My friends in the office purchased a card and gift for me. That gift was an album of hymn arrangements, sung by Fred Waring's Pennsylvanians! The very album I had wanted and had crossed off the prayer list. The amazing fact was that I had not conveyed that desire to my colleagues at work!

God was evidently saying in a very personal way, "Did you really think that I care only about your *needs*? Did you think your *wants* were unimportant to me? I delight in providing for the wants of my children, especially when they delight themselves in obeying and following me!"

God leads by specific instructions in His Word.

GOD LEADS THROUGH SANCTIFIED REASON

Two churches were asking virtually the same thing. They wanted someone to come to serve them for approximately six months as an interim pastor, while they were searching for their permanent pastor.

One of the churches was located near Rochester, Minnesota. The other was located in Anoka, Minnesota. The Rochester opportunity came from an established church whose pastor had moved. The Anoka request came from a Bible study group that met in a home for the mid-week service, and in a school on Sundays.

Accompanied by my family, I went to both of these places to see what they were like. In a family conference we discussed both churches, and we prayed about the choice we had to make.

I made a list of the pros and cons of each situation. I tried to analyze the personalities of the two churches to see where my type of ministry would fit in better.

The final choice was made on the basis of careful reasoning, backed by earnest prayer that we would not make a mistake. God did not guide us in any dramatic way. The decision was based upon logic and analysis, and personal choice. All of these were backed by prayer, of course.

That the choice we made was the correct choice became evident over the next eight years, as we watched that small group of people in Anoka grow into one of the sturdiest churches on the north side of the city of Minneapolis. During that six months elongated into eight years, we had the joy of seeing a beautiful, sprawling church complex erected on a 55 acre campus! A Christian school was established that now numbers over 300 in attendance. The missionary giving climbed to nearly $100,000 a year. The Lord was greatly honored through this "little group," and as we look back, we realize that we could not have made a better choice, even if God had given us a vision to direct us, or had spoken from heaven in an audible voice saying, "This is the way, walk in it!"

It may have been a case of God saying, "*You* decide. I am pleased to have you serve me wherever you choose." Because we were careful

131

to remind Him in the midst of that choice that if He had a specific choice for us, we were more than willing to follow that direction, He may have decided to place His hand upon that Anoka work in a phenomenal way.

Sometimes we are to use our own sanctified reason. We are to make our own decisions, when God has not given specific instructions.

(Note: I have only told a part of the story here, the part that illustrates making a choice through sanctified reason. Later in this section, I will tell you the rest of the story to illustrate yet another point.)

GOD LEADS THROUGH THE COUNSEL OF GODLY PEOPLE

The pastorate on Long Island was full of challenge and delight for me as a young pastor, yet in the back of my mind from time to time there arose a desire to help prepare other pastors someday, at one of the Bible colleges.

There were a couple of obstacles in the road to a teaching profession. I did not have a master's degree, and I knew that it was minimal for such a position. The church I was pastoring was able to pay us very little, and there were no funds available to pursue higher education, even on a part-time basis.

The desire persisted. One day, while visiting the campus of Nyack Missionary College, I met Dr. Harry Hardwick on the road that winds through the campus. The warmth of the personal interest of that man of God had always delighted me. To have a few moments to chat with him there would have made my day quite apart from the far-reaching implications that conversation was to have!

Dr. Hardwick is always keenly interested in you, no matter who you are! He enquired about my activities, my dreams, my future. It has never been difficult for me to be open with a man like that. When he knew of my desire to teach in a Bible college, he suggested that I think of New York University for my further training. It was within easy reach of my present pastorate. Finances might not be a problem, he suggested, if I would apply for a scholarship. He would be glad to give them a reference.

I had never even thought of the possibility of a scholarship. He encouraged me to aim high. "Ask them for an entire semester's tuition!" he urged. Inspired by the counsel of my godly friend, I made the application, and then prayed about the results. To my amazement, the university sent me a scholarship that would cover my entire master's degree program!

The counsel of a godly friend had been used of the Lord to prepare me for the years I would enjoy at the St. Paul Bible College as Dean of Students, and as an assistant professor of Homiletics and Pastoral Methods.

A further delight, like whipped cream on the pie, was that when I was prepared to apply for the position, my friend Dr. Hardwick had become the president of the St. Paul Bible College! I had the great joy of serving for nine years under his

133

inspiring leadership in a teamwork concept that made those years among the happiest of my life.

Yes, God leads through the counsel of godly people.

GOD LEADS THROUGH
DEVOTIONAL APPLICATION

Earlier in this section I mentioned the Anoka congregation that we served, after having made the choice between it and a congregation in Rochester, Minnesota. What I did not tell you was that after the six-month agreement had been fulfilled, the board asked us to stay on as their permanent and full-time pastor.

I could not see that as a possibility, since I was teaching full-time at the St. Paul Bible College, and was not really considering taking an independent church. I even had a suspicion that certain beliefs that I held to be especially precious in the Word of God might not be held by those people. I had never tested those beliefs there, for I felt one should avoid any controversial subject when serving as an interim. As a permanent pastor, I would have to preach the whole counsel of God. We might find a conflict in our beliefs at certain points.

Repeatedly the board told me that they had prayed seriously about the matter, and they were convinced that God would have us stay on with them. As gently as possible, I discouraged the idea. When I reminded them that God had not told *me* that we should remain there with them, one of the board members said somewhat facetiously, "Pastor, you're just not listening!" We laughed together, and I dismissed the idea from my mind. After all, I *did* want the will of God for my life—there was no question about that. That issue had been settled long before then. It was common sense that told me, for a number of reasons, that this was not a permanent place for us to serve.

Some months later, with the people still pressing for an affirmative decision, I realized that the only way to get them to look seriously for someone else to serve them was for me to submit an official resignation. I did that. Once again they assured me seriously that they had sought the mind of the Lord and felt He was prompting them to ask us to stay. How kind of them! But again, I tried to dismiss the idea on the basis of all the logical considerations.

In the meantime, God allowed certain changes to take place that made me begin to question whether we were to remain in education, or return to the pastorate. My friend, Dr. Hardwick, had accepted an invitation to go to be the President of LeTourneau College in Longview, Texas. My urge to serve a congregation grew increasingly over the months. I began to take seriously certain invitations that were received, but did not consider the place where I was preaching each Sunday, in spite of their urgings.

One day, feeling the need of direction from heaven, I prayed earnestly that God would give us some word that would lead us. I was reading in the book of Isaiah (where my bookmark was for that day) and I came to the words, "Who is blind but my servant, and deaf like the messenger I send? Who is blind like the one committed to me, blind like the servant of the Lord? You have seen many things, but have paid no attention; your ears are open, but you hear nothing." [110]

I stopped reading right there. That board member's remark came back forcefully, "Pastor, you're just not listening!" It was no joking matter now! "Lord, I'm not trying to be deaf. You know that. I want Your will above everything else!" I prayed.

I won't go into the details, but in the next few chapters the Lord spoke in ways that fit our situation so specifically that I felt He was indeed telling us we were to serve that congregation that we had turned down so many times.

To be certain of that, there would have to be other kinds of divine confirmation. But the ball was rolling now, and it gained momentum rapidly.

I called for a meeting of the board and very honestly explored with them the areas I felt my beliefs might conflict with theirs. My body had been miraculously restored to health and usefulness when certain death lay ahead. There was no way I could avoid preaching the thrilling truths in the Bible concerning God's ability to heal. I felt they would not agree with that.

"Pastor, we know what the fifth chapter of James teaches!" one of the board members assured me. He was surprised that I would even think that they would disregard that plain teaching. It was like that with each objection I listed for them. At the end of the board meeting, I knew we would be serving that congregation for some years. God had made it plain.

How had He made it plain? Initially through devotional application; specific statements in the Bible had arisen out of my systematic devotional reading. God has used this method time and time again to direct me, or to reconfirm His leadings in my life. Because God has used this method more than any other method in my life, I want to add yet another illustration out of my personal experience, before I go on to another category.

After desperately searching for living quarters during post World War II years, God made available to us the attic of a large home on Walnut Avenue in Cranford, New Jersey. There were dormer windows on each of the four sides of that house there in the attic. One dormer area had been made into a tiny bathroom, and the rest were all open into the center of that one large room. The entire area had been beautifully paneled. We could make one alcove into a living room. Another could be a bedroom. A third could be the kitchenette, and we could cook on a hotplate or in a dutch oven.

I cannot describe to you the sense of relief I felt as the head of that little family the day we moved into that large attic room. Nor can I tell you how great was the joy I felt when my devotions that night confirmed that we were there in the will of God.

My bookmark was in the Psalms, and in the course of my reading I came to a verse that had never impressed me in my previous readings.

"Thou hast set my feet in a large room," it read. [111] I have since lived in some lovely, spacious places in the course of God's leadings, but never have I had a sweeter consciousness of being exactly where God wanted, and had put me, than that night, kneeling by my bed in that "large room."

I believe that God loves to speak to us through our devotional reading. I believe that the Christian who neglects his daily quiet time with the Bible and with his Lord, does so to his own impoverishment.

GOD LEADS BY OPEN DOORS

No amount of human logic could have directed me to Bible school the year I went as a young man. There were no savings on hand. My parents and I were poorer than church mice, as I look back upon it. Oh, we didn't feel that way. Those were exciting days of trusting God for *everything*!

I filled out the application for Nyack Missionary College by faith. "How much will you have on hand when you enroll?" the application questionnaire asked. It didn't say whether I was supposed to answer that question realistically, or by faith, so I chose the latter. I wrote down $500 in that space, not knowing where one cent of it would come from. How I wished I had written $1,000, for when registration day arrived, I had precisely $500 that God had sent to me in response to that act of faith!

During those years at the Nyack Missionary College, I was as frugal as any student they ever had. I answered people's letters only if they included a stamp! I did not visit the popular "Hub" to buy treats and snacks. I relied totally on "care packages" for those.

Increasingly, however, I felt a desire to take voice lessons in order to improve my ministry in my home church, and in my travels with my roommate, Doug Herbert. Doug was an excellent chalk artist, and I sang and played as background music for his drawings.

It did not seem right, however, for me to use $25 for that luxury when I was trusting God for my necessities. I prayed, "Lord, if You want me to take those lessons, would You send $25 in one lump sum, so that I will know that You intend it to be used for them?"

The day after Christmas one of my Sunday School boys, David Crane, came to the door of our attic apartment and handed me a Christmas card. In it was a note that said, "We cut down the big Colorado spruce tree in front of our house, and I made it into wreaths and sold them. I want you to have the money." I praised God for His faithfulness, and rejoiced over this specific answer to prayer (a gift of exactly $25!).

A wealthy widow heard about this while I was home on my Christmas vacation. She gave me an additional $10 saying that she wanted it to be used for the rental of a practice room, or anything else that might arise in the way of additional expenses. I told her that I was quite certain that there was no rental fee for use of a practice room, but she insisted that I receive her $10 anyway.

When I enrolled for the lessons, the registrar asked me if I had any preference for a teacher. I did indeed! I wanted Miss Geraldine Southern. "Are you aware," he asked me, "that Miss Southern's lessons are $35 for a semester? The other teachers' are $25." No, I wasn't aware of that, *but God was*. How amazing! God had known from the beginning that my need was for $35 and not for $25. He also knew that if He were to send me that $35 in one gift, I would not have used it for voice lessons. In His marvelous love, He had sent first the $25 and then had prompted another of His faithful ones to add $10 to that, so that I might have Miss Southern as my teacher.

By doors opened so graciously, God had led.

GOD LEADS THROUGH THE GIVING OF AN INNER PEACE

"Peace I leave with you; my peace I give unto you. I do not give to you as the world gives. Do not let your hearts be troubled and do not be afraid" (John 14:27).

I can hardly think of a more universally cherished possession than peace! In the center of the circle of the will of God there is a perfect peace.

Sometimes God confirms our decisions through a deep-seated inner peace that is a very subjective kind of thing. If it is not present, we ought to reevaluate the decision, and run it

140

through careful scrutiny once again.

When that peace is there, we can move forward with strong confidence, even in the midst of adversities and reverses. When God led Elaine and me to open a new church at Commack, on Long Island in New York State, we did it because of very specific instructions given to us in our devotional reading. There were other confirmations as well. We were so certain that we were in the will of God that when, after six months of serving there, we had a Sunday when there were only six people in attendance at the services, we felt not one twinge of discouragement. A year later we would be having more than 100, but even though we could not foresee that, His peace that passes understanding was ours because we *knew* we were there in the will of the Lord. That very peace became a further confirmation to us!

So deeply subjective is this way by which the Lord leads, that it is difficult to illustrate. Paul and Silas, *singing* in the prison, with their feet fast in the stocks, and their backs bleeding from the beating they had received, is probably the most vivid illustration we can envision!

GOD LEADS IN A VARIETY OF WAYS

No list of ways by which the Lord leads could possibly be complete. God is greater than man's lists, and His love for variety is everywhere illustrated.

I will conclude this book with a few unusual

God-given directives that defy classification. We will see how an unusual circumstance, a lapse of memory, a traffic light, a startling name slipped into my mouth, were all used of the Lord to give direction.

A young bachelor pastor gets invited out to eat quite often, especially in the homes of those who have eligible daughters! I was just finishing the Sunday noon meal in such a home in Brooklyn, New York, when the ring of the phone proved to be a call for me. "Pastor Shepson, the lights will not work here at the church, and we are preparing for the Spanish service. Can you help us?" the lady asked.

I left the table and hurried to the church. The first thing I checked was the fuse box. Everything seemed to be all right. I threw the main switch to the "off" position and then back to the "on" position again. Immediately the lights came on! "Pastor, we had tried that many times and nothing happened!" exclaimed someone standing by watching.

I lived across the street from the church, so instead of returning to the home where I had been a dinner guest, I went over to my apartment. The moment I walked in through the door, my phone started to ring. It was Jimmy Jones, a young Roman Catholic catechist with whom I had been studying the Bible in private sessions. "I am so thankful you are home, Pastor," he said. "I came to this phone booth and before dialing, I prayed, 'God, if you are as real as Pastor Shepson seems to believe, please, *please* let him be home right now. I need to talk to him so badly.' ''

Through unusual circumstances God had directed me back to my apartment so that I would be there in answer to that young man's earnest prayer. His perfect will for my life for that moment was brought about by His own definite intervention.

God's resourcefulness is further illustrated in this next vignette: My anthropology class was finished at the University of Minnesota. I hurried out of the stale air of that classroom, and made my way down to the street. I followed the crowd of students toward the edge of the campus, and hurried toward my parked car, nearly twelve blocks away. There was *so* much to be done back at the office, and I wanted to get there as quickly as possible.

Nearing my car, I suddenly realized with disgust that I had left my notebook back in the classroom! Feeling a deep frustration, I spun on my heel and headed back toward Ford Hall. At least twenty blocks of unnecessary delay because of my stupid carelessness! I hurried toward that final traffic light, quickening my pace with the realization that it could turn red at any moment. Just as I neared the curb, the light changed to red. Inwardly I fumed!

At that point, Romans 8:28 came to mind. Does even the changing of a traffic light that blocks your path when you are in a hurry fit into God's blanket statement that everything is for our good? I pondered that momentarily, and then the light turned green for me again. I hurried on across the street. Somehow I was conscious of a

footfall directly behind mine
pace with mine. I slowed
correspondingly. I turned t
young man I didn't know

"Aren't you in my
questioned. "With Dr
He nodded. "Yes,
preacher, aren't you
did you know?" I
you were carryin
said. With tha

"Wait a mi
that God m
corner for
and we
yoursel
to att
thro

me, "Oh, Pastor, when you said, 'the Gililand family,' I knew that God was talking to me. My name is Wanda Gililand!" God had chosen to slip a name into my mouth, to fulfill His perfect will! How I wish this were the norm rather than the exception!

There is no real end to this book. God is working daily in marvelous ways, to reveal to His own the perfect plan He has for their lives. Our lives are very carefully planned for us. There is nothing that can touch us within the circle of His will that is not either sent from God or permitted by Him. Even our disappointments are His appointments.

The more confident you are of that, the more meaningful and satisfying your Christian life will be. My prayer is that God will let this book be just a starting point for you in a new and deeper experience of implicit trust and confidence, coupled with implicit obedience. If that happens, you will be the richer...*and so will God!*

NOTES

Section I

1. Bill Bright, "Knowing God's Will is Not a Guessing Game," March 1976 issue, *Worldwide Challenge*, Campus Crusade for Christ, Inc.
2. Paul Little, *Affirming the Will of God* (Downers Grove, Ill.: InterVarsity Press, 1971), p. 3.
3. Ibid., p. 6.
4. A.W. Tozer, "How the Lord Leads," (Harrisburg, Pa.: Christian Publications).
5. Romans 8:14, *The Holy Bible, New International Version* (Grand Rapids, Michigan: Zondervan Bible Publishers, 1978). Note: All Scripture passages are quoted from this translation of the Bible unless otherwise noted.
6. I Samuel 13:14.
7. Poem, author unknown.
8. I Corinthians 3:11-15.
9. John 14:15.
10. Colossians 1:9,10 (RSV).
11. Deuteronomy 28:1,2.
12. Dwight Carlson, *Living God's Will* (Old Tappan, New Jersey: Fleming H. Revell

Company, 1976), p. 23.
13. J. Sidlow Baxter, *Does God Still Guide?* (Grand Rapids, Michigan: Zondervan Publishing House, 1968), p. 109.
14. Hebrews 6:17.
15. Ephesians 2:10.
16. Bill Bright, "Four Spiritual Laws," (Campus Crusade for Christ, Inc., 1965) p. 2.
17. Psalm 32:8.
18. Isaiah 30:21.
19. Romans 12:2.
20. Bill Bright, "Knowing God's Will is Not a Guessing Game," March 1976 issue, *Worldwide Challenge*, Campus Crusade for Christ, Inc.
21. Elisabeth Elliott, *Shadow of the Almighty* (New York: Harper & Brothers, 1958), p. 166.
22. Revelation 12:11,12.
23. Donald Grey Barnhouse, *Let Me Illustrate* (Old Tappan, New Jersey: Fleming H. Revell Company, 1967), p. 340.
24. Basil Miller, *George Muller* (Minneapolis, Minnesota: Bethany Fellowship, Inc., Copyright 1941, by Zondervan Publishing House), p. 50.
25. Donald Grey Barnhouse, *Let Me Illustrate* (Old Tappan, New Jersey: Fleming H. Revell Company, 1967), p. 342.
26. Paul Little, *Affirming the Will of God* (Downers Grove, Ill.: InterVarsity Press, 1971), p. 10.

Section II

27. Numbers 22:21-31.
28. Acts 10:9-20.

29. Bill Bright, "Knowing God's Will is Not a Guessing Game," March 1976 issue, *Worldwide Challenge*, Campus Crusade for Christ, Inc.
30. Ibid.
31. F.W. Faber.
32. Author unknown.
33. II Corinthians 6:14.
34. Jeremiah 17:9.
35. Matthew 19:6.
36. II Peter 3:9.
37. I Thessalonians 4:3.
38. Romans 8:29.
39. Acts 15:19.
40. M. Blaine Smith, *Knowing God's Will* (Downers Grove, Illinois: InterVarsity Press, 1979), p. 21.
41. John 15:7.
42. Psalm 37:4.
43. I John 5:14.
44. Margaret Erb, "God Has a Plan," *Essays on Guidance* (Downers Grove, Illinois: InterVarsity Press, 1968), p. 7.
45. Paul Little, *Affirming the Will of God* (Downers Grove, Illinois: InterVarsity Press, 1971), p. 22.
46. Acts 15:28.
47. I Peter 1:24, Colossians 3:16 (note especially Today's English Version), Hebrews 4:12 (note especially the New English Bible).
48. Psalm 37:3 (K.J.V.).
49. Psalm 37:16 (K.J.V.).
50. II Samuel 2:1 (L.B.).
51. Revelation 3:7,8.
53. Saint Paul Bible College (Bible College,

149

Minnesota) motto.

54. Oliver Barclay, *Guidance* (Downers Grove, Illinois: InterVarsity Press, 1978), p. 37.
55. Margaret Erb, "God Has a Plan," *Essays on Guidance* (Downers Grove, Illinois: InterVarsity Press, 1968), p. 11.
56. Ibid., p. 9.
57. Frances R. Havergal, "A Worker's Prayer" (hymn).

Section III

58. II Samuel 12:27 (L.B.)
59. Ezra 1:2 (L.B.)
60. Ezra 7:20 (L.B.)
61. I Chronicles 11 (chapter heading in N.I.V.)
62. I Chronicles 17:4,8,10.
63. I Chronicles 17:16.
64. I Chronicles 17:18-20.
65. I Chronicles 22:7,8.
66. II Chronicles 6:7.
67. Rev. Irving Malm, District Superintendent for the Western District of The Christian and Missionary Alliance. Letter of April 6, 1979.
68. Rev. Elmer B. Fitch, District Superintendent for the Midwest District of The Christian and Missionary Alliance. Letter of January 23, 1979.
69. Rev. Robert J. Gould, District Superintendent for the Canadian Midwest District of The Christian and Missionary Alliance. Letter of June 29, 1979.
70. Psalm 17:14.
71. Psalm 104:6-23 (excerpts) (L.B.).
72. James 4:2.

73. Matthew 19:29.
74. Isaiah 44:2,8 and Isaiah 49:11-13.
75. II Timothy 2:13.
76. Basil Miller, *George Muller* (Minneapolis, Minnesota: Bethany Fellowship, Inc., copyright 1941, by Zondervan Publishing House), p. 18.
77. Isaiah 65:1.

Section IV

78. Margaret Erb, "God Has a Plan," *Essays on Guidance* (Downers Grove, Illinois: InterVarsity Press, 1968), p. 12.
79. Robert Oertler, Jr., "Undebatable Guidance," *Essays on Guidance* (Downers Grove, Illinois: InterVarsity Press, 1968), p. 26.
80. Carl Thomas, "Good...Acceptable...Perfect," *Essays on Guidance* (Downers Grove, Illinois: InterVarsity Press, 1968), p. 37.
81. Oliver Barclay, *Guidance* (Downers Grove, Illinois: InterVarsity Press, 1978), p. 47.
82. Paul Fromer, "How to Design an Automobile," *Essays on Guidance* (Downers Grove, Illinois: InterVarsity Press, 1968), p. 33.
83. Donald Grey Barnhouse, *Let Me Illustrate* (Old Tappan, New Jersey: Fleming H. Revell Company, 1967), p. 340.
84. Robert Oertler, Jr., "Undebatable Guidance," *Essays on Guidance* (Downers Grove, Illinois: InterVarsity Press, 1968), p. 28.
85. John 7:17.
86. Margaret Erb, "God Has a Plan," *Essays on Guidance* (Downers Grove, Illinois: InterVarsity Press, 1968), p. 6.

151

87. Bill Bright, "Knowing God's Will is Not a Guessing Game," March 1976 issue, *Worldwide Challenge*, Campus Crusade for Christ, Inc.

88. Margaret Erb, "God Has a Plan," *Essays on Guidance* (Downers Grove, Illinois: InterVarsity Press, 1968), p. 10.

89. Luke 11:13.

90. James 4:2.

91. James 1:5 (L.B.).

92. James 1:6-8 (L.B.).

93. Psalm 48:14.

94. Hebrews 11:6.

95. Margaret Erb, "God Has a Plan," *Essays on Guidance* (Downers Grove, Illinois: InterVarsity Press, 1968), p. 10.

96. Keith Samuel, "I Felt Led," *Essays on Guidance* (Downers Grove, Illinois: InterVarsity Press, 1968), p. 51.

97. I Kings 19:11,12.

98. I Kings 18:45.

99. I Kings 17:22.

100. I Kings 18:38.

101. Robert Oertler, Jr., "Undebatable Guidance," *Essays on Guidance* (Downers Grove, Illinois: InterVarsity Press, 1968), p. 25.

102. Basil Miller, *George Muller* (Minneapolis, Minnesota: Bethany Fellowship, Inc., Copyright 1941, by Zondervan Publishing House), p. 103.

103. Mark 4:38.

104. Acts 27:14, 20, 25.

105. Basil Miller, *George Muller* (Minneapolis, Minnesota: Bethany Fellowship, Inc., Copyright 1941, by Zondervan Publishing House), p. 51.

106. The New Testament, *The Confraternity of*

Christian Doctrine Edition (Patterson, N.J.: St. Anthony Guild Press, 1941), p. 1.

Section V

107. Used by permission of the Slavic Gospel Association, P.O. Box 1122, Wheaton, Illinois, from the Fall 1978 issue of their news magazine.
108. James 4:2.
109. Psalm 34:10 (K.J.V.).
110. Isaiah 42:19,20.
111. Psalm 31:8 (K.J.V.).

BIBLIOGRAPHY

Barclay, Oliver R. *Guidance: What the Bible Says About Knowing God's Will.* 5th edition. Downers Grove, Illinois: Inter-Varsity Press, 1978.

Baxter, J. Sidlow. *Does God Still Guide?* Grand Rapids, Michigan: Zondervan Publishing House, 1968.

Bayly, Joseph, et. al. *Essays on Guidance.* Downers Grove, Illinois: InterVarsity Press, 1968. Contributors include Margaret Erb, Robert Adams, Robert Oertler, Jr., Paul Farmer, Carl Thomas, Keith Samuel, Alice Bittner, Kenneth Geiser, Kenneth Pike, Mildred Cable, Eugene Nida, Richard Webster, Jane MacMurray.

Bright, Bill. "Knowing God's Will is Not a Guessing Game." *Worldwide Challenge*, Campus Crusade for Christ, Inc. March 1976.

Carlson, Dwight L. *Living God's Will.* Old Tappan, New Jersey: Fleming H. Revell Company, 1976.

Flynn, Bernice and Leslie Flynn. *God's Will—*

You Can Know It. Wheaton, Illinois: Victor Books, 1979.

Howard, J. Grant, Jr. *Knowing God's Will and Doing It.* Grand Rapids, Michigan: Zondervan Publishing House, 1976.

Jauncey, James H. *Guidance by God.* Grand Rapids, Michigan: Zondervan Publishing House, 1969.

Little, Paul E. *Affirming the Will of God.* Downers Grove, Illinois: Inter-Varsity Press, 1971.

Nelson, Marion. *How to Know God's Will.* Chicago, Illinois: Moody Press, 1963.

Smith, M. Blaine. *Knowing God's Will: Biblical Principles of Guidance.* Downers Grove, Illinois: Inter-Varsity Press, 1979.

Tozer, A.W. "How the Lord Leads." Pamphlet. Harrisburg, Pennsylvania: Christian Publications, Inc.

White, John. "Guidance," chapter 8 of *The Fight.* Downers Grove, Illinois: Inter-Varsity Press, 1976.